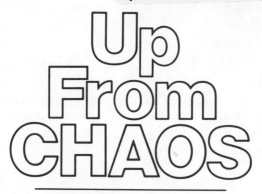

Up From CHAOS

GENESIS TODAY

by LeRoy Lawson

You may obtain a 64-page leader's guide and a 32-page activity book to accompany this paperback. Order numbers 40071 and 40072 from Standard Publishing or your local supplier.

A Division of Standard Publishing
Cincinnati, Ohio 45231
No. 40070

Scripture quotations are from the *Revised Standard Version,* © 1946 and 1952, unless otherwise indicated.

Library of Congress Catalog Number 78-62706
ISBN 0-87239-235-X

Printed in U.S.A.   1979

Table of Contents

God Is in Charge Here

Genesis 1 and 2

"A man has no reason to be ashamed of having an ape for his grandfather."

This was Thomas Huxley's famous reply to Bishop Wilberforce in their creation-evolution debate before the British Association for the Advancement of Science meeting at Oxford in June, 1860. Huxley was defending the heretical view of Charles Darwin, who claimed man evolved from primitive forms of life. Wilberforce stood on the more traditional belief that man is the result of a special creative act of God.

One clergyman returned home from the meeting and told his wife of Huxley's horrifying assertion that man was descended from the apes. His wife is said to have exclaimed, "My dear! Descended from the apes! Do let us hope it is not true; but if it is, let us pray that it will not become generally known."

The rumor has, however, become widely known. The scientific community has generally accepted evolution as a working hypothesis, although there is little agreement about the precise manner and form of evolutionary development. The average citizen has remained unconvinced. So the debate between "godless evolution" and Biblical creation has continued to this day.

But there are signs that the hostilities may be cooling off. A recent *Time* essay entitled "Science: No Longer a Sacred Cow," discusses the new doubts about scientific achievement and a growing uneasiness within the scientific community.

A later issue of *Saturday Review* devotes several pages to a special section entitled. "God and Science: New Allies in the Search for Values." The section does not address all the issues, but it does suggest that science and religion are now listening to each other with a new humility, each hoping to learn from the other. Now that scientists can so readily destroy and alter life, many of them realize they must join with religion in the quest for value, meaning, and truth. Science, they admit, cannot provide all the answers necessary for the survival of civilization on this globe.

In this newly humble spirit many scientists are now reading the Genesis account of creation without prejudice, and to their surprise they are discovering it does not teach that everything began exactly 4004 years before Christ (as Bishop Ussher announced in the seventeenth century), that it does not deny a developing creation from simple to complex, and that it does not oppose many of the insights of science.

Let's see what Genesis does say about creation.

It says that *God is*.

"In the beginning God . . ." With these simple words the Bible sets forth its statement of faith. It makes no attempt to prove the existence or character of God. It merely accepts that *He is* and *He does*.

Had the ancient Hebrew been asked, "How did you get here?" he would have answered without hesitation, "God put me here." And there the discussion would have ended. He would not have speculated that some blind force operated upon the universe to bring it—and him—into existence. He would have laughed at the suggestion that chance could have formed the solar system and that natural selection or the survival of the fittest alone could have accounted for his life. He was not the hapless victim of his heredity or environment. "In the beginning God ..." meant to him that all existence, including his own, is ruled by a Being with personality, power, and purpose.

Our Hebrew ancestor could not have explained God; indeed, he would have thought it presumptuous of anyone to try. But he would have had no doubt that God existed, that He created heaven and earth, and that He was still very actively involved with His creation.

At the very beginning of time, then, when nothing else was, God was. And today, in the midst of time, God is.

Genesis states further that *God said*.

"Let there be light ..."

Again we note the simplicity of the Biblical narrative. While affirming that the earth was willfully created by an intelligent and powerful Creator, it does not detail the ingredients of creation. Its point is that *the God who is* is a *God who can speak* life into existence, by whatever means He chooses.

By the word of the Lord the heavens were made,
and all their host by the breath of his mouth
. . . .
Let all the earth fear the Lord,
let all the inhabitants of the world stand in
awe of him!
For he spoke, and it came to be;
he commanded, and it stood forth.
—Psalm 33:6, 8, 9

The word He spoke contained His will and expressed His power. "By faith we understand that the world was created *by the word of God* . . ." (Hebrews 11:3).

The word of the Lord came to a world waiting to be born, and it was born.

(And the Word of the Lord later came to men and women waiting to be reborn, and those who received Him were reborn—John 1:12.)

Genesis leaves no doubt that God brought the world into being through His willful creation. But when God said, "Let there be . . ." He said no more. Genesis asserts that God did it, but does not say how. I'm glad it doesn't. Any explanation that could accomodate the level of scientific knowledge of one age would be inadequate to the level of another. It is far better that Genesis portrays the drama of creation without irritating us with all the stage directions. I agree with Christopher Morley's opinion:

I went to the theater
With the author of the successful play.
He insisted on explaining everything;
Told me what to watch;
The details of directions,
The errors of the property man,
The foibles of the star.
He anticipated all my surprises
And ruined the evening.
Never again! And mark you,
The greatest author of all
Made no such mistake.[1]

Like Morley's playwright, theologians and scientists have made many mistakes trying to force the Genesis account to say more than it does. The sparse narrative leaves room for human imagination to fill in the gaps; and that is good, provided we do not then insist that all other Christians accept our imaginative interpretations or be labeled heretics.

The Bible says that *God said*.

And that *God ordered*.

He spent six creation days forging chaos into order. When the Spirit of God moved over the face of the waters, He began His step-by-step process of ordering and establishing the universe according to His purposes.

Out of the void, form
Out of the blackness, night and day
Out of the spaces, heavens and earth,
   stars and sun and moon.
Upon the planet, creatures of the sky
   seas and land,
Reproducing after their kind, in genetic
   order.
Then man.

The simplicity of Genesis vividly contrasts with the complexities of most evolutionary theories, which teach that living creatures became what they are today by chance, without an ordering intelligence in charge.

But how could a chance evolution of life happen? Biologist Edwin Conklin has been quoted as saying that "the probability of life originating from accident is comparable to the probability of the unabridged dictionary resulting from an explosion in a printing shop."[2]

Cressy Morrison, in *Man Does Not Stand Alone*[3], gives this explanation. He asks us to take ten pennies and mark them from one to ten, then return them to our pocket. Now draw them out in sequence from one to ten, putting each coin back in the pocket after each draw. We have one in ten chances of drawing number one first. The chance of drawing one and two in succession would be one in 100; one, two, and three in succession would be one chance in 1000. The probability of drawing one through ten in the correct order is one chance in 10,000,000,000.

Just think, then, of the fantastic mathematical probabilities involved in placing the planet earth exactly the right distance from the sun to support life.

The earth rotates on its axis in twenty-four hours, or at the rate of a thousand miles an hour. Suppose, asks Mr. Morrison, that it turned at a hundred miles an hour? This would make the days and nights ten times as long as they are now, long enough to burn the vegetation by day and freeze it at night.

Even the earth's twenty-three degree tilt is essential to maintain vegetation. Otherwise we should have continents of ice at the poles with deserts in between.

The examples could be multiplied endlessly. There is no need. We can readily see that it requires a greater stretch of faith to believe that all the requirements to support life on earth came into being through mindless chance than to believe that God with superhuman intelligence deliberately arranged this life-support system according to His divinely conceived purposes. The Bible says *God ordered it*.

One fact Genesis makes very clear about the newly created world: *God liked it.*

Do you remember James' Weldon Johnson's poem?

And God stepped out on space,
And he looked around and said:
I'm lonely—
I'll make me a world.

And as far as the eye of God could see
Darkness covered everything,
Blacker than a hundred midnights
Down in a cypress swamp.

Then God smiled,
And the light broke,
And the darkness rolled up on one side
And the light stood shining on the other,
And God said: That's good!

Then God reached out and took the light in his
hands,
And God rolled the light around in his hands
Until he made the sun;
And he set that sun a-blazing in the heavens.
And the light that was left from making the sun
God gathered it up in a shining ball
And flung it against the darkness,
Spangling the night with moon and stars.
Then down between the darkness and the light
He hurled the world;
And God said: That's good.[4]

Johnson may have missed one or two of the finer
shadings of theological interpretation, but he is right
about one point; God liked what He had made.

The world was not inherently evil; matter was not
bad, nor were man and woman blemished as God
created them.

When His creative work was accomplished and in
leisure God surveyed His handiwork, He knew what He
had created was good. He liked it.

Notes

[1]"No Coaching," from *Streamlines*. J. B. Lippincott Company ©
1933, 1934, 1935, 1936, by C. Morley. Reprinted by permission.

[2]Quoted in "Nine Scientists Look at Religion," *Readers Digest*,
January 1963, p. 92. (From *The Link*, November 1962. © by The General Commission on Chaplains and Armed Forces Personnel.)

[3]New York: Fleming and Revell Company, 1944, chapter 1.

[4]From GOD'S TROMBONES by James Weldon Johnson, Copyright
1927 by The Viking Press, Inc. Copyright © renewed 1955 by Grace
Nail Johnson. All rights reserved. Reprinted by permission of Viking
Penguin Inc.

In God's Image— What Difference Does It Make?

Genesis 1:26-31; 2:4-9

The basic question in the first chapter was, "How did we get here?" God put us here, we answered, by a special creative act. We are not here by accident; neither are we the natural result of a mindless evolutionary process. "In the beginning God created the heavens and the earth"—and us.

The record says He created us to be *in his own image.* But what does that mean, we ask, and what difference does it make?

A psychologist assures us that our self-image makes all the difference in the world. A primary task of every counselor is to help his patient develop an adequate self-concept. He not only asks, "Who are you?" but he also must ask, "Who are you trying to become?" That is, what is the image that you are trying to achieve?

During the civil-rights demonstrations in the mid-sixties, a white woman watched disapprovingly as more than fifty white Alabamans marched alongside a much larger host of blacks in Selma. "Just what do they want?" she asked.

An elderly black woman standing nearby answered her. "We just wants to be treated like people," she said.

Like people. She has an image of what human beings are supposed to be. Like the rest of us, she has two pictures of herself: what she is and what she would like to become. It is the second picture that shapes our future and moves us to action.

It therefore makes a great difference in whose image we think ourselves to have been made. What we see as we look at the image strongly influences the kind of persons we become. Will Rogers, defending a friend who had recently brought much criticism on himself, insisted, "You can't tell what a man is when you are looking at him. You don't know what he sees. You have got to get around behind him and see what *he* is looking at."[1]

Perhaps an extreme example of this truth is Joey, the Mechanical Boy. Ignored as a baby by parents who didn't want him, Joey was fed, changed, toilet-trained, and in every way treated according to a rigid, mechanical schedule. Since neither his mother nor father really wanted anything to do with him, Joey became convinced that machines were better than people. So he thought of himself as being made in the image of a machine, and he began to function like one. When he was hospitalized as a sickly-looking nine-year-old, he carried his imaginary wire with him from room to room. He had to be plugged in in order to run. When he sat at the table, he "insulated" his body with paper napkins before plugging himself in; only then could he eat. When he slept he devised contraptions from masking tape, cardboard, and whatever else he could scrape up; these kept his body-machine working through the night. In the bathtub, he rocked back and forth with engine-like regularity, splashing water all over the floor. When he wanted to, he could become deathly still, like a switched-off machine. The hospital had a long, three-year struggle to bring Joey back to reality, to convince him that he had been made a person, not a mechanism.[2]

Joey's case is extreme, of course. But he illustrates a general truth. We are shaped by our self-images. That's why it matters in whose image we are made.

Some teach us that *we have been made in the image of machines*, not in Joey's sense, but in an equally shocking one. The writings of Red China's Mao Tse-tung teach that doctrinaire communism values men primarily as pieces in a vast social machine. They have no inherent worth as individuals; their importance is the contribution they make to the goals of the party. They are tools, manipulated by their leaders.

If man is a machine it really doesn't matter how you tamper with him, if your tampering makes a more efficient society.

Some see us as made *in the image of animals*. After all, they say, we share the lower primate's skeleton and other physical characteristics. Our behavior can be observed in orangutans, chimpanzees, and gorillas. We can be stimulated to make predictable responses like white mice in mazes. And we fight for our territory like birds and beasts. Really, Nietzsche said, "I am not much more than an animal which by means of blows and tidbits hath been taught to dance."

If we see ourselves as mere animals, driven by instincts, slaves of our bodily functions, then we have no right to ask people to live according to a high moral code or to be fair and reasonable to one another. The depraved, dissolute, frequently disgusting man of contemporary literature and film is all we can expect of man made in the image of animals.

A more recent image is *the computer*. Some leading thinkers in our time speak freely of programming human behavior just as we program a highly sophisticated computer. Read such books as *Games People Play* and other popular psychologies and you'll find the language of computer programming, as if our brains were tapes that record all inputs of data to be stored in memory and "printed out" when stimulated.

Many students of human behavior believe the genes have already written our program, and we are just playing out the role our heredity has predetermined for us. They claim that all human behavior—morality and justice, immorality and crime, spitefulness, leadership, affection—is dictated by our genes. Others give a little more credit to the shaping forces of our environment, including of course toilet training and home atmosphere. B. F. Skinner has taught that if we can totally control a child's environment from birth, we can control his behavior as an adult.

In what image is man made? Is it in the likeness of the machine, the animal, the computer? When I ask, 'What is man?' or more personally, 'Who am I?' where do I go to find the answer? A linguistics expert said that if he were inquiring into human nature, "I'd be out interviewing bartenders and cab drivers and prostitutes. They see a lot more of human nature than I do."[3] But do they? What is it they see? It is obvious that this linguist has an understanding of man very different from the Bible's, and it is not a very elevating one.

Neither is Henry Morgan's definition of a kleptomaniac. A kleptomaniac, he quips, is "a person who helps himself because he can't help himself." But if he is an animal, or a machine, or a computer, he cannot help himself in anything he does. Neither can we.

By now I've said enough to make the point: it matters what image we think ourselves patterned after.

That is why it is so important to understand the teaching of Genesis that *man is made in the image of God*.

Image implies both likeness and difference. It suggests a man's peculiar dignity upon earth at the same time it reminds us not to think too highly of ourselves. A man is not God, although he in some ways resembles God. When he thinks he is God, he sins. When he obeys and imitates God, he becomes his best self.

In the image of God means that man is not a machine. He must not be owned and manipulated and used for the advantage of someone else.

In the image of God means that he is not an animal, driven by instincts and lusts.

In the image of God means that man is not a computer, incapable of thinking for himself or charting his own course in freedom.

In the image of God means *like God*, but *not God*. Man is unique upon earth. He may physically resemble some of the animals, but he is more than they. He is not a god, however, because he is limited in mind and body.

He is man. There is none other like him.

He is of the earth: "Then the Lord God formed man of dust from the ground." Analyze his body and you will find the common chemicals of our planet; dissect his anatomy and you will discover bones, blood vessels, nerve structure, and bowels much like those you see in other primates. He is dust, and to dust he shall return.

But he is more than the earth: "Then the Lord God . . . breathed into his nostrils the breath of life." When God filled the man with godly breath, what was less than animal became more than animal; what was of the earth became of Heaven too. Unlike the animals, man has to look up, beyond the earth, to discover what he really is.

He is the highest of earthly creatures. He has dominion (Genesis 1:26).

He is the manager of his portion of God's estate. "The Lord God took the man and put him in the garden of Eden to till it and keep it" (Genesis 2:15). He has a vocation: he is a steward of what God has given him to manage.

He is responsible for his freedom. He is free to eat or not eat of the tree of knowledge of good and evil. God leaves the choice—and the consequences of the choice—with him.

This is man: an intelligent, resourceful, infinitely important creature of God.

But one thing he does not have. He does not have independence. He is only in the image of God, he is not God. He is still in the earth, bound by its laws and dependent upon God's provisions. He is a God-breathed soul, a creature of Heaven, aspiring to be like God, but he does not know all God knows and therefore cannot free himself of God, except on peril of his life.

Thus *image* means "like God" but "distinct from Him." Just how important is this image?

In every man there lives an image
Of what he ought to be.
As long as he is not that image
He ne'er at rest will be.[4]

That's how important.

But since the image has become tarnished through man's fall, (Genesis 3), how can we know what we really are supposed to look like? How can we imitate God? Colossians 1:15 declares that Christ "is the image of the invisible God, the first-born of all creation." There's the answer. *To become like Christ* is to bear the image of God. "Just as we have borne the image of the man of dust, we shall also bear the image of the man of heaven" (1 Corinthians 15:49).

Christians, then, pattern their lives after Jesus Christ, believing Him to be the clearest image of God this earth has ever seen, for, unlike Adam, He did not fall. He came to rescue and restore a world of human beings whom God made after His own likeness.

What difference does all this make? Perhaps the best answer comes in a letter attacking Christianity in A.D. 178. Celsus, a bitter enemy of Christianity in the second century, struck at the heart of the Christian religion: "The root of Christianity," he wrote, "is its excessive valuation of the human soul, and the absurd idea that God takes an interest in man." Celsus was right. When Genesis says that God made us in His own image, it holds the human soul to be of infinite worth, a fact that Christ later proved on the cross. Charles Spurgeon summarized the Biblical view of man as briefly as possible: "God has no time to waste making nobodies."

Today's secular critics of Christianity cannot accept the Bible's evaluation of man's worth. They argue that we are merely temporary eruptions on a small planet in an insignificant galaxy, hardly worth God's attention, if indeed there is a God.

But if there is a God, and if He created the heavens and the earth, could He not have created a unique race upon this planet, a race with some of God's own attributes, so that we might love and communicate with Him? Isn't this possible?

I believe so.

The Bible says so.

Notes

[1] Daniel A. Poling, *Mine Eyes Have Seen*. New York, Toronto, London: McGraw-Hill Book Company, Inc., © 1959, pp. 279, 280.

[2] *Scientific American*, March 1959. Condensed in *The Reader's Digest*, June 1959.

[3] Ward Cannel and June Macklin. *The Human Nature Industry*. Garden City, New York: Anchor Books, pp. 45, 46.

[4] By Friedrich Ruckert. Quoted in Helmut Thielicke, *The Freedom of the Christian Man*, Grand Rapids: Baker Book House, 1963, p. 32.

Sin's Hangover

Genesis 3

That man is a sinner is obvious enough. A century that has survived the horrors of two world wars, concentration and refugee camps, Korea and Vietnam needs no further proof that we have been driven from Paradise. America, the land of the free and brave, is also the home of the demonic, the pervert, and the criminal. We need no psychoanalyst to convince us that deep within there is a blackness, a dark underside that contradicts our respectable public faces.

The overwhelming evidence of human sinfulness makes Genesis 3 an easy Scripture to believe. The fall of Adam and Eve is our story. We have lived it. Genesis 1 and 2 proclaim a world made by God, a good world. God made man and woman in His image and gave them a paradise to enjoy. Then they spoiled everything. The message is quite clear: though the serpent tempted them, the fault was their own. Their sin was a rebuke to God: " We don't like where You put us, God. You made us higher than animals, that's true, but not equal with You." They wanted to be more than He made them; they wanted forbidden knowledge. They wanted to be God, to rule their own destiny, to sever their dependency upon Him.

It isn't that they were ignorant of God's will. They just didn't fully believe in Him. By trusting the serpent more than God, they separated themselves from Him. God spoke; they rebelled. They thought they knew better than their Creator.

This and succeeding chapters chronicle what they lost. We shall read of their expulsion from the garden, their bondage to the soil, the murder of brother by brother, the nearly universal degeneration of the human race and the consequent flood . . . and on and on. The pages of the Bible (and of all history) evidence the damage man has inflicted on himself because he persistently obeys his tempter instead of his God.

Genesis 3 illustrates sin's damage. Our loss is fivefold.

Through sin *we lost our innocence*. Before their fall, Adam and Eve did not know fully the difference between good and evil. They were genuinely innocent, at ease with God, with their world, with one another. They had no reason to cover their bodies with hides or leaves. But when they sinned, they needed secrecy. By disappointing God they had disappointed themselves and could face neither God nor themselves without shame. So they hid their lost innocence.

We still hide behind our clothes. Innocent little toddlers may be able to run about without anything on, but we cannot. Stripped naked, the blemishes on our bodies reflecting the stains on our souls, we lack the covering by which we try to impress our neighbors. So we cover up, not only to be less exposed, but also to look more like what we want people to think we are. We discriminate among men, in fact, by their clothes. We even think we can tell the good guys from the bad guys by their coverings of cloth.

This fact horribly struck a young observer at the Auschwitz trial in 1964. Like most of us who lived through or studied World War II, he thought of the Nazi Gestapo as the very embodiment of evil in human flesh. Their inhuman atrocities against the Jews during the war shock the imagination. What the young man saw at the trial shocked him even more, however. The presiding judge politely conducted a trial noted for its dignity and propriety. The defendants, who were charged with the slaughter of thousands of prisoners, were not at all what the young observer expected. He had anticipated seeing men in stiff black uniforms and high riding boots, with clubs or whips in their hands and black looks on their mean faces. But at the trial these men looked no different from anyone else. In their civilian clothes, they looked just like him.

Was it possible that he who so closely resembled the defendants would also have been capable of their brutality? He felt innocent when he could identify the SS uniform and be sure that all who wore it were evil. But when he saw the men without the uniform, could he ever again feel immune to the temptations that caused their fall? Can it it be that beneath our uniforms we are all alike?

Can we then really feel superior to Adam and Eve, having simply replaced their fig leaves with our wrinkle-free fibers?

No, we have *all* lost our innocence.

And our *closeness to God*. The serpent told Eve, "God has lied to you. You will not die." When Eve accepted the serpent's words as truth, she trusted him more than God. When she and Adam tasted the fruit, they rejected God's authority over their lives. They walked away from their closest friend.

When God called, "Where are you?" He was beginning Adam's lesson in sin's consequences. "You have left me, Adam," He was telling him. "You have run away and hidden from me. You have broken a trust and destroyed our intimacy. Once you were near me and with me, but you were not satisfied with our relationship, so you left me. Now where are you? With whom have you replaced me?"

Sin is more than a breach of a rule, such as breaking the Sabbath or withholding a tithe or telling a lie. It is withdrawing from God, breaking the close tie with which God wants to hold us in His love. Dr. Karl Menninger, the famed psychiatrist, calls this separation from God "another word not only for sin, but for mental illness, for crime, for nonfunctioning, for aggression, for alienation, for death."[1]

The inevitable consequence of withdrawing from God is a *loss of the sense of personal responsibility* that makes us human. God had given Adam and Eve dominion over every living thing that moves upon the earth, including themselves. But as soon as they turned against God they quickly denied their responsibility and began blaming someone else. "It's the serpent's fault," Eve pleaded. "She made me do it," Adam defended himself. Their excuses are as modern as my children's earnest declaration yesterday that they had not cluttered up the family room. (It's amazing how that room is so often in disarray, but nobody has ever done it!)

We are so adept at blaming someone else for our sins that some writers claim the fault in the first sin was not really the serpent's, nor Adam's and Eve's, but God's. If He had not made them weak, the argument goes, our ancestors would not have succumbed to the temptation.

But read the chapter carefully. Although God cursed the serpent for wrongly tempting the man and woman, He nevertheless respected Adam and Eve enough to punish them. "You could have resisted," He told them in effect. "I created you strong enough to resist the

22

serpent's subtle murmurings. I must therefore hold you responsible."

They did not like His approach, of course. The sinner's theme song has always been, "It's not my fault." Here are some modern renditions of the song:

• A few years ago seven men were hauled into court and charged with causing six thousand dollars worth of damage to a rented house during a coming-out party in Long Island. One of the boys, who crash-landed a chandelier he was swinging on, explained that they had been drinking for two days. He was willing to admit that "someone has a moral obligation" for the damage, but didn't know who was responsible. It was clear, however, that he was sure it was not his fault.

• In Chevy Chase, Maryland, a tenant who fell behind on his rent offered this inventive excuse: the leak in his living room had given him an ailment that paralyzed his check-writing arm at rent-payment time!

• In New Zealand a woman who had been driving without a license for twenty-five years explained to the judge that she drove on roads with very little traffic, and none of those roads led to an office where she could apply for a driver's license.

• In marriage counseling, I seldom hear either the husband or the wife say, "It's my fault. I'm responsible." It's always the spouse's problem.

• All ills in our government, we note, are the fault of the *other* party, or the *other* branch of government. (To the White House, it's always Congress' fault; to Congress, the Administration erred.)

• All wars in history have been started by the *other* side. Theirs is all the evil; justice resides with us.

We don't need to extend the list. The fact is that our rebellion from God lowers self-esteem and heightens insecurity. We insist that others be more responsible than we want to be. We are like children who say, "It got lost." Maturity will admit, "I lost it."

With our loss of personal responsibility *we also lose our freedom*. We hand our lives over to those persons or agencies to whom we grant responsibility, and then we fear them as they control us. "No man is free who is not master of himself," Epictetus, a slave, wrote many centuries ago. Adam and Eve handed the serpent their responsibility. He then became their master. They lost the freedom God had granted them, and anxiety took over. "I was afraid . . . I hid."

No man who is not at peace with God is at peace with himself. He is not free.

In no society whose members are not at peace with one another can freedom survive. They must be regimented. They are not free.

Ours has been called an age of anxiety, our country a nation of sheep, our culture a wasteland, our time a lost generation. We have lost our freedom.

And without freedom, we *lose our sense of being at home here*. Adam and Eve literally lost their home; we share their experience in our pervading feelings of rootlessness and restlessness. We are wanderers, always seeking but never finding. For present-day Adam the soil becomes hostile, thorns and thistles replace fruited trees, happy cooperation gives way to sweat and struggle.

When you were younger and disobeyed your parents, didn't you say, "I can't go home. I can't face Dad"? Then, to justify yourself, didn't you eventually add, "It's his fault anyway"? Didn't you lose your home—or your feeling of being at home?

When you fell from the image of God, didn't you say, "I can't go back to church. I can't listen to those sermons and have to examine myself"? Then, to justify yourself, didn't you say, "The church is full of hypocrites anyway"? Didn't you lose your church home?

When we have sinned, we don't want to face God. But since this is all God's world, where do you go when you have withdrawn from God? You are no longer at home in Paradise.

These, then, are the losses of Adam and Eve. They are our losses, too, for

> The Lord looks down from heaven upon the children of men,
> to see if there are any that act wisely,
> that seek after God.
> They have all gone astray, they are all alike corrupt;
> there is none that does good, no, not one.
>
> (Psalm 14:2, 3)

What shall we do then? Shall we give up?

No, because there is one thing Adam and Eve did not lose: *they did not lose hope.* The hint is given in verse 15. The serpent may bruise the heel of the future generations of man, but man will find a way to bruise the head of the evildoer.

Another hint is given in verse 21. "And the Lord God made for Adam and for his wife garments of skins, and clothed them." Covering their shame and their need, God continued His history-long care for His own.

A third hint opens the next chapter. Eve rejoiced in the birth of Cain, saying, "I have gotten a man *with the help of the Lord.*"

And so the story goes through the rest of the Bible. God hovers over His children, not ever permanently forsaking them. And one day He gives them the greatest hope of all, one like them but not like them, called Christ, to lead them over the thorny soil of earth to a new dwelling place, where once again they can live intimately and joyfully with their God.

Notes
[1]*Whatever Became of Sin?* New York, Hawthorn Books, 1973, p. 190.

Am I
My Brother's
Keeper?

Genesis 4:1-16

Genesis does not say why Cain's vegetable offering was inadequate. Hebrews 11:4 names Abel among the giants of faith, implying that his animal sacrifice showed his faith in God, while Cain's offering from the field did not. First John 3:12 says that Cain "was of the evil one" and "his own deeds were evil and his brother's righteous." Several guesses about the offering have been made through the centuries, but Genesis does not say.

In fact, Genesis is not interested in that part of Cain's story. It points to another moral, one that makes us very uneasy. We would rather speculate about God's unspoken reasons for rejecting Cain's sacrifice than face up to the undeniable answer to Cain's question.

"Am I my brother's keeper?" is his frightened effort to deflect God's piercing gaze. As his parents hid from God behind their fig leaves, Cain tries to hide behind a screen of words. God does not directly answer, because He doesn't have to. In the brief sixteen verses of this passage, *brother* appears seven times. We can quibble over whether Cain is Abel's "keeper" if we want to, but we cannot deny his obligation to Abel, his *brother*.

Cain's experience parallels that of his parents in many ways.

Both events begin with the sin against God. Adam and Eve insult Him by their disobedience, Cain does so with his inadequate offering.

Having failed God, they turn against one another in their retreat from Him, Adam accusing Eve, Eve blaming the serpent, and Cain attacking his brother.

They suffer the penetrating questions of God. To Adam and Eve God says, "Where are you? Who told you that you were naked? What is this that *you* have done?" To Cain He says, "Why are you angry, and why has your countenance fallen? Where is Abel your brother? What have *you* done?"

The final question to each is God's insistence that He had made them strong enough to act responsibly. The parents cannot blame the serpent for their own failure. The son is warned, "If you do well, will you not be accepted? And if you do not do well, sin is couching at the door; its desire is for you, but you must master it." For God to tell us that we must master temptation is assurance enough that we can overcome it if we will.

Even Cain's losses parallel those of his parents. He too loses his innocence. His murder leads to his dishonesty ("I do not know") and his impudence ("Am I my brother's keeper?"). Secrecy, the sign of lost innocence, invades his life as it has his parents'. He can no longer be open about what is in his heart.

He loses his intimacy with God. "Then Cain went away from the presence of the Lord . . ."

He loses his sense of personal responsibility. "I am not accountable for my brother's death," he tries to

27

tell God. But God, who has already heard human excuses, holds him responsible. In the fall of Adam and Eve, God teaches them that He expects responsibility for their actions. In His lesson to Cain, the emphasis shifts. To personal responsibility God now adds family obligation. "Abel is your brother, therefore your responsibility."

He loses his freedom also. Fear grips him. He who has dwelt in peace with his family and fields now sees enemies everywhere. To fear the Lord is to have no other fears; to leave Him is to leave His protection and become captive to anxiety.

He loses his home. "I shall be a fugitive and a wanderer on the earth . . ."

But again, like his parents, he does not lose everything. He has hope. God does not let go of him completely, but places a special protective mark on him, warning away would-be assailants.

Cain's experience is thus a deepening and broadening of that of his parents. Their fall was in relation to God's will. His is a sin against both God and man. To be fully human is to live in intimate fellowship with God and in harmony with man, accepting obligations to God and brother.

Thousands of years later mankind's greatest teacher would cut through the snarled undergrowth of Jewish laws and call all men to learn the lessons God taught our first parents and their erring son:

> You shall love the Lord your God with all your heart, and with all your soul, and with all your mind. This is the great and first commandment [the lesson to Adam and Eve]. And a second is like it, You shall love your neighbor as yourself [the lesson to Cain] (Matthew 22:37-39).

Yes, we are our brother's keeper.

Who, then, is our brother? I have always liked the answer of the old rabbi who was asked by one of his students, "Rabbi, why did God only make two people in the beginning?"

"That's so no one can ever say, 'I come from better stock than you come from.'" We are all one large family, then, all brothers and sisters. The Bible makes it pretty clear the human race is one race. We belong to one another whether we like it or not. In spite of subsequent divisions, God initially meant us to be united.

One thing is certain. We are dependent upon one another. Consider Leslie Weatherhead's illustration of our need for one another:

> When I rise and go to my bath a cake of soap is handed me by a Frenchman, a sponge is handed me by a Pacific Islander, a towel by a Turk, my underclothes by one Englishman, my outer garments by another. I come down to breakfast. My tea is poured out by an Indian or Chinese. My porridge is served by a Scottish farmer, or my corn flakes by Mr. Kellog and his friends. My toast I accept at the hands of an English farmer who has joined hands with a baker. My marmalade is passed to me by a Spaniard, my banana by a West Indian. I am indebted to half the world before I have finished breakfast.[1]

And the day has just begun.

We learned during the depression of the 1930's that the world's national economies are completely interdependent. When one fell, they all fell. On a more local level, no community can function without the voluntary cooperation of mutually responsible men and women who know, to some degree at least, that they are their brothers' keepers.

Within the church the family feeling is even more intense. The church is called, among other names, a body (with all the members functioning and essential to the health of the whole), a household of God (a large family), a royal priesthood (with every believer a priest offering himself as sacrifice for others, following the high priest Christ). We are intimately brothers and sisters within the church.

But we also are related to men and women outside the church. What is Jesus teaching in the parable of the good Samaritan (Luke 10:29-37) if not that all men and women should be the objects of our brotherly love? We are truly members one of another—intimately so within the body of Christ and generally so throughout the race.

Proof of our interrelatedness came to this country in 1947 in the person of a Mr. LeBar of Mexico. A Mexican importer, Mr. LeBar travelled from Mexico to New York City to conduct his business. He did not know that he was carrying a fatal smallpox infection. He created a panic in the city by spreading the disease wherever he went.

Perhaps we need this proof of our interrelatedness and mutual dependence, because popular opinion teaches just the opposite. "Look out for Number One" is today's most popular doctrine. The extreme to which we push this belief can be seen in one man's prison experience in World War II. Elie Wiesel struggled with his obligation to his fellow man—in this case his aged, ailing father. He watched helplessly as the old man slowly lost his battle for life in the filth and cold of their prison. The head of his block, watching Wiesel's desperate attempts to help his father, put his hairy hand on his shoulder and gave him this counsel:

Listen to me, boy. Don't forget that you're in a concentration camp. Here, every man has to fight for himself and not think of anyone else. Even of his father. Here, there are no fathers, no brothers, no friends. Everyone lives and dies for himself alone. I'll give you a sound piece of advice—don't give your ration of bread and soup to your old father. There's nothing you can do for him. And you're killing yourself. Instead, you ought to be having his ration.[2]

Secretly Wiesel wanted to agree with him. He knew it was too late to save his father and he wanted the rations of bread and soup. But something higher called him, and he continued to take care of the dying man.

Some would call him foolish, because they believe that life is like that concentration camp. For them, there are "no fathers, no brothers, no friends." It is every man for himself. We are nobody's keepers.

Often we hear warnings that we shall all soon be facing this issue. With the world's population rising at an alarming rate, it is feared that the global food supply will not be able to feed the masses. Already some experts are advising America to turn her back on the underdeveloped countries. They use the argument of "lifeboat ethics." America, they say, has plenty of food because of our natural resources, limited birthrate, and wise management of the agricultural economy. In a sea of undernourished human beings, our countrymen are like survivors in a lifeboat. The sea is filled with millions begging to get into the boat; but if we let them all in (that is, if we try to feed them all), the boat will sink and everybody will be lost. Therefore we must preserve the lives of those in the lifeboat. Those in the sea must drown.

Am I my brother's keeper?

In the troubled days of the fifties and sixties, many of our national leaders were encouraging us to construct bomb shelters. And many were built. A friend of mine began making preparations for his family. He told me of his shelter and the stock of food he was preparing. He could care for his family's needs for many months if necessary, he said.

He was very proud of his plan until I asked him one question. "What about your neighbors who can't make these preparations?" He curtly replied, "They aren't my worry. Let them take care of themselves as I have taken care of me and my family."

He has probably forgotten the incident. But I haven't, because I still have neighbors and brothers. And I am still asking, "Am I my brother's keeper?"

At my house lives a woman whom I love very much. I guess there's nothing I wouldn't do for her.

And three children live there. I love them, too, and would do just about anything for them.

I have some very good friends. They know that I am prepared to do all I can for them.

Now let me see—are there any others I would call "brother"?

What makes me uncomfortable is to recall that Jesus said God loved the whole world and sent Him to save as many as would turn to Him. His love for these "brothers" cost Him His life. Jesus' disciples, their teacher told them, would also have to take up crosses.

There is no way around it: I am my brother's keeper . . . or at least his brother.

I must review my list again. I love my wife, my children, my good friends, my . . .

Lord, do you mean it? Are they *all* my brothers?

Notes

[1]*Salute to a Sufferer* by Leslie Weatherhead. New York, Nashville: Abingdon Press, © 1962, p. 35.

[2]A selection from NIGHT by Elie Wiesel, translated from the French by Stella Rodway. © Les Editions de Minuit, 1958. English translation © Mac Gibbon & Kee, 1960. Reprinted with the permission of Hill and Wang (now a division of Farrar, Straus & Giroux, Inc.).

The First and Final Cleansings

Genesis 6—9

The early chapters of Genesis are a chronicle of God's disappointments. First Adam and Eve broke His heart. Then Cain. Then the whole human race. "The Lord saw that the wickedness of man was great in the earth, and that every imagination of the thoughts of his heart was only evil continually. And the Lord was sorry that he had made man on the earth."

Human rebellion against God was now complete. Even basic decencies were abandoned. What had begun in the garden with one man and one woman infected their sons and daughters generation upon generation, until God could tolerate mankind's wickedness no more. "I will blot out man whom I have created from the face of the ground . . ."

There was nothing else to do. Man had already lost everything else. There was no innocence any longer. Gone was man's intimacy with his Creator; gone also was any sense of personal responsibility. Fear had replaced freedom, and restlessness moved through a race that could not feel at home any more. There was nothing left for man to lose but life itself. So with disappointment God prepared to cleanse the earth.

As soon as we say that God was disappointed, however, we must hasten to add something else: He was not totally disappointed. There was that one man, Noah, shining like a diamond among counterfeits, who found favor in the eyes of the Lord. "Noah was a righteous man, blameless in his generation." He walked with God.

We have trouble explaining Noah. How do you account for a good man? For centuries philosophers have struggled with the problem of evil, wondering how a good and powerful God could allow the presence of evil in His creation. Another question, however, is equally problematic: in a race so obviously devoted to wickedness, how can a man emerge who is so different from the norm, whose standards are righteous? Where did he learn his goodness? How could he resist the pressures of his peers?

We ask these questions because we know one thing for certain. Wickedness is contagious, and only the spiritually powerful can resist it. Leo Tolstoy, lamenting his wild youth, recalls the ease of his fall into sin with familiar words.

> I desired with all my soul to be good; but I was young, I had passions, and I was alone, wholly alone, in my search after goodness. Every time I tried to express the longings of my heart to be morally good, I was met with contempt and ridicule, but as soon as I gave way to low passions, I was praised and encouraged.

Who can't remember his adolescence, when friends sniggered at him for attending worship or refusing to be "one of the boys" in the beer or pot parties? Tolstoy continues:

Ambition, love of power, love of fame, lechery, pride, anger, vengeance, were held in high esteem. As I gave way to these passions, I became like my elders, and I felt that they were satisfied with me.[1]

So even now children grow up in a moral atmosphere far to the east of Eden. Unlike Noah, we have been infected, so we await the judging waters.

The sparse narrative of Genesis does not explain Noah's righteousness. It just describes his moral character and God's choice of him to carry the human race through the flood.

The Bible frequently slows the pace of its narrative to present a brief biography of a single individual, as if to illustrate repeatedly that it is God's way to choose one man or woman to serve all His people. We think in terms of committees or governments; God seems instead to lift up individual personalities whose influence can turn the course of history. Noah was such a man.

I asked a friend of mine to name the one personality in the twentieth century he considered the greatest example of personal influence. He immediately named Mahatma Gandhi of India. Gandhi was not a Christian, although he often expressed his admiration for Christ's life and teachings and acknowledged his debt to Christ. On March 12, 1930, this nearly naked little man, dressed only in loincloth and with no weapon but his unwavering commitment to his understanding of the will of God, left Sabarmati to march to the sea. His goal was to violate the government's monopoly by extracting a bit of salt. He knew he would precipitate a crisis. He intended to, for he had a higher goal: to free India from the British Empire.

You know the rest of the story. Seventeen years later this little man, standing alike against the might of the

British and the violence among his own people, accomplished his goal.

In this respect, one man against the many, Noah has had many descendants. Totally committed, they brave the taunts of the disbelieving multitudes in order to obey what they are convinced is the voice of God. What we may forget is that we ourselves have the same potential influence that Noah exercised.

God did not make us to be nobodies. He relies upon our influence, and from time to time He enlists one of us to perform a rescue mission for Him. He does not arm us with sword or rifle. He uses instead what He has given all His people—an influential personality. Everybody who matters to anybody has that power.

Through one man God saved the race. Think what He might do through us!

With Noah as His redeeming agent, then, God commenced to cleanse the earth. "I will blot out man . . ." His purpose was not destruction, but purification. He did not desire to obliterate the whole human race, but to start again, to give His children another chance. This He did by burying man's past in order to raise a new creation with a new hope. This experience became so strongly etched in human imagination that many centuries later the letter of 1 Peter compared the water of Christian baptism with the waters that saved Noah and his family (3:21). These are purifying waters, separating the righteous from the unrighteous.

What causes the reader to meditate on the flood story, however, is the vision of death and destruction as the raging floods overwhelm the helpless hordes. For those not held in the hand of God, judgment is awful.

Easy conscienced Americans, trained to believe in tolerance as the supreme virtue, find the Biblical language of judgment offensive. Although we would deny our affinity with the culture of India, in almost every section of America these words of a Hindu scholar express our belief: "God is one, and the paths are many ... God welcomes us in whatever way we approach him, and for each man that religious tradition is best in which he is born and bred."

But what if we are born into a tradition of wickedness? Is that best for us? Suppose we are born into a tradition of error. Is that better than truth? Some are born to despair. Is that preferable to hope?

How can we say that all paths lead to God, that each religion is equal to every other?

The Bible certainly does not agree with that comfortable opinion. It teaches that not all ways lead to Heaven, that not all beliefs are acceptable to God, that there will be judgment and destruction. The ark carried eight to safety, but left the multitudes to drown.

The apostle Paul's vision of the end likewise pictures terrible judgment:

when the Lord Jesus is revealed from heaven with his mighty angels in flaming fire, inflicting vengeance upon those who do not know God and upon those who do not obey the gospel of our Lord Jesus. They shall suffer the punishment of eternal destruction and exclusion from the presence of the Lord and from the glory of his might (2 Thessalonians 1:7-9).

The final book of the Bible warns that "if any one's name was not found written in the book of life, he was thrown into the lake of fire" (Revelation 20:15).

We cannot escape this fact. The Bible speaks of sin and its consequences, of separation and judgment, and of destruction. When God cleanses the earth, He cleanses it thoroughly.

But the salvation of Noah and his family showed that God's purpose was not destruction, but rescue. There

37

was rain, but there was also the rainbow. The floods covered the earth, but the ark rode the waves of the flood. God rescued the righteous.

That was the first cleansing. Another is coming. "While the earth remains, seedtime and harvest, cold and heat, summer and winter, day and night, shall not cease." This is God's promise to Noah that there will be no more all-encompassing floods. But with the promise is the plain suggestion that the earth will not remain forever. Once the earth began, and sometime the earth will end. And when that day comes, the Bible teaches, there will be another cleansing, another separating of the righteous from the unrighteous.

We don't really need the Bible to teach us that our existence is shaky. Ultimate human destiny may remain a mystery without the Bible, but consequences of our human condition are present everywhere. The world's two superpowers now have the nuclear capability to obliterate all life from the face of the earth. We know enough of mankind's darkened heart to see a real probability that they will do exactly that. In a moment, in the twinkling of an eye, one demented ruler can touch the fatal button.

Then the lake of fire.

To bring about the final cleansing God will not have to do anything but leave us alone.

Jesus himself spoke of the end, and He used the experience of Noah to make His point.

But of that day and hour no one knows, not even the angels of heaven, nor the Son, but the Father only. As were the days of Noah, so will be the coming of the Son of man. For as in those days before the flood they were eating and drinking, marrying and giving in marriage, until the day when Noah entered the ark, and they did not know until the flood came and swept them all away, so will be the coming of the Son of man. Then two men will be in the field; one is taken and one is left. Two women will be grinding at the mill; one is taken and one is left. Watch therefore, for you do not know on what day your Lord is coming (Matthew 24:36-42).

What then should we do?

We should believe in the God who controls the floods and fires.

We should trust in the God whose hope is to rescue, not to lose, the human race.

We should obey the voice of the one who orders an ark to be built, even as the noise of the disbelieving crowds rings in our ears.

We should be ready, for we don't know the day or hour.

The day of the Lord will come like a thief, and then the heavens will pass away with a loud noise, and the elements will be dissolved with fire, and the earth and the works that are upon it will be burned up. Since all these things are thus to be dissolved, what sort of persons ought you to be in lives of holiness and godliness, waiting for and hastening the coming of the day of God . . . (2 Peter 3:10-12).

What sort?
The believing, trusting, obeying, ready sort.
Like Noah.

Notes
[1]Taken from LIFT UP YOUR EYES: The Religious Writings of Leo Tolstoy. Edited by Stanley R. Hopper. Copyright © 1960 by The Julian Press, Inc. Used by permission of Crown Publishers, Inc.

The Abandoned Tower

Genesis 11

To understand what went wrong at Babel we need to remember what Genesis 1 says about God.

In the beginning God created the heavens and the earth, and He has never relinquished His authority over His creation. He spoke, and the universe appeared. Out of chaos came order, and out of the void came life. And when He had finished His work, God surveyed what He had accomplished and He liked it. It was good.

Adam and Eve thought they could improve upon God's order. They paid for their presumption.

Cain took the power of life and death into his own hands. He too paid for his presumption.

Noah's contemporaries had so far abandoned God that even their imagination became perverted. God had no choice but to abandon them.

The citizens of Babel are simply following the footsteps of their ancestors. Having forgotten God, they are building a monument to their own impressiveness.

And they really are impressive. It is easy to forget that many human virtues are exhibited at Babel. After all, these men are building a city. Consider the complex cluster of qualities required for men and women to live in close quarters harmoniously. We may admire (and rightly so) the ingenuity required for a farmer to till the land, tend his flocks, repair his machinery, and provide for himself and others; but in fairness we must also give due credit to the makers of cities.

Think of the necessary cooperation required to provide adequate distribution of food and other goods, to supply heat, light, water, and sewage disposal for thousands of people. We may complain about inadequate housing, but it takes a certain collaborative genius to provide any housing at all for masses of people. The supporting agricultural system and the economic systems in cities are marvels of human invention. The legislative, judicial, and executive branches of local and regional governments may not always function to our liking, but without them daily life would break down. And our cities—not our rural regions—have provided cultural achievements that have led the human race to greater and greater accomplishments. Think of the arts, sports, sciences, and technological achievements of the cities, and you'll have to admire the virtues of urban dwellers.

I recently was asked to give a series of lectures on the urban church. I did so gladly. I like preaching in the city and I recall that the heaven awaiting us wears the name of a city: the new Jerusalem.

The citizens of Babel are also capable of constructing a tower. They are led by architects and engineers of note. One has only to visit the pyramids of Egypt or the Coliseum of Rome—or marvel over the hundreds of miles of Roman aqueducts—to realize that the twentieth century does not hold a monopoly on architectural ability.

One other virtue must be noted. So much could be accomplished at Babel because the people there spoke one language. They were not fragmented by a multiplicity of foreign tongues. Without linguistic unity, harmony among people is more difficult.

But now I want to note that the one language consisted of a few words, as the Revised Standard Version translates Genesis 11:1. We can make too much of this fact, of course, but a few words precisely chosen are superior to many words with slippery shades of meaning. Jesus was critical of men who heap up empty phrases in their praying, thinking that they will be heard for their many words. He taught His followers instead to pray briefly and simply (Matthew 6:7-13). An example He presented was a man who, afraid even to lift his eyes before God, could only ask God to "be merciful to me a sinner" (Luke 18:13).

Jesus taught us to pray simply, "Give us this day our daily bread." Someone translated that brief request into the language of the legal profession:

> We respectfully petition, request, and entreat that due and adequate provision be made, this day and the date hereinafter subscribed, for the organizing of such methods of allocation and distribution as may be deemed necessary and proper to insure the reception by and for said petitioners of such quantities of baked cereal products as shall, in the judgment of the aforesaid petitioners, constitute a sufficient supply thereof.

A people flooded with such verbosity cannot help thinking the citizens of Babel were virtuous in their few words.

But of course the sin of Babel, not the virtue, is the reason Genesis records its abandonment. Babel's sin is the dominance of *us*: "Let *us* build *ourselves* a city ... make a name for *ourselves*." No mention of God, no recognition of His authority.

The subtle staying power of this sin is evident in the advice we still give a young man when he leaves home. We wish him well, but we tell him to go out and make a name for himself. We don't really mean to do it, but we encourage his pride and prepare for his downfall. The Christian does not make a name for himself. When he is converted to Jesus Christ, he receives a new name. He doesn't make one. From that moment on, whatever he does, in word or deed, he does to glorify the name of God (1 Corinthians 10:31).

We could call Babel's failure the sin of self-sufficiency. God does not judge them because they are building a city or tower, but because they are doing all for self glory. They believe they are sufficient. They think they do not need God.

In the winter of 1978, much of the United States was battered by blizzards. Just prior to the one that hit Indianapolis, the Department of Transportation announced, "We are prepared." For several years the DOT had been bitterly attacked by residents of Indianapolis for its inability to deal with the increasing snowstorms that had marked Indiana's winters. So, for the 1977-78 winter, the DOT assured the residents, there would not be a major problem.

Then the worst winter of recorded history hit. The city was paralyzed. The downtown area was closed. For days only a few vehicles braved the drifted streets. In one of the city's black churches the minister saw the hand of God in the blizzard as a direct answer to the DOT. "You may think you are prepared," God was saying to the Department of Transportation, "but I've sent the snow to remind you that I am still in charge, I'm still God, and you aren't self-sufficient. You cannot be totally prepared."

Theologians may debate the fairness of the preacher's interpretation of the Indianapolis shutdown, but the Bible leaves no doubt that the incident at Babel was God's way of saying, "You are not self-sufficient. You cannot replace me. I am still God."

In the Babel incident, men as a whole proclaimed their self-sufficiency apart from God. Our contemporary sin is that we believe ourselves to be individually self-sufficient, wanting neither God nor man to help us. Contemporary self-help books quickly become best sellers. They encourage us to *Win Through Intimidation*, to be *Looking Out for Number One*, or to exercise our own *Power*. The message in many books is the same. You don't need anybody else. You have all the power you need within your individual personality.

Marlon Brando illustrates the extreme to which this philosophy can be carried. He bought himself an island, Tetiaroa, thirty miles north of Tahiti. There he provided every conceivable comfort for himself and his family. His justification for his self-indulgence? "I'm convinced the world is doomed. The end is near. I wanted a place where my family and I could be self-sufficient and survive."

Doesn't that sound like Babel? "Let us be self-sufficient, like the gods."

During the middle ages many religious hermits, in an excessive desire to save themselves—and without any concern about the salvation of others—devoted themselves to earning their place in heaven. One hermit passed sixty years without seeing or speaking to another human being; another one habitually practiced standing like a crane upon one leg until he fainted. The hermit's message was clear: "This is my way of being religiously self-sufficient and of saving my own soul." A man may make a name for himself just by avoiding other men, but there is no record that God praises such long-term loneliness.

The religion of the hermits was a type of self-worship. The retreat of Brando is another form of self-worship. The self-sufficiency proclaimed by Robert Ringer's *Winning Through Intimidation* and *Looking Out for Number One* is yet another variation of the same theme. When C. S. Lewis was asked which of the religions gives its followers the greatest happiness he answered, "While it lasts, the religion of worshipping oneself is best." No doubt he's right.

But it cannot last.

For God is still God.

His punishment is to attack the citizens of Babel at the point of their greatest strength. They have spoken with one intelligible language. "Let us . . . confuse their language, that they may not understand one another's speech." When they could no longer communicate with one another, their building project was over and the citizens of the shattered city were scattered.

The text says that the Lord confused their language, making it impossible for them to understand one another. They may have been speaking in different tongues, or they may have been speaking the same words but not understanding them. Many of us who speak English are aware that we cannot always understand other English-speaking persons. They may speak with different dialects or accents. They may use words unknown to us, or use familiar words with different meanings. We can travel from one part of the United States to another and encounter real difficulties of understanding.

While aboard an airplane recently, I read an article in the airline's magazine on this problem of communication within the English language. Having listed many of our problems, including the use of technical jargon, euphemisms, snobbery, and other means of clouding the language, the author concluded thus:

The biggest cause of these sins of discommunication is thinking about oneself instead of the audience. Ego is singular, likely to be massaged in solitude. Communication is plural, involving interaction with others, and makes it possible to win over multitudes. Ego is the enemy of good communication.[1]

We've already concluded that the sin of Babel was ego (another name for self-sufficiency). When one concentrates on himself, he finds it impossible effectively to communicate with another.

Ego is the source of suspicion, jealousy, rivalry, class distinctions, and secrecy. Because they are all looking out for number one, bosses develop certain secret languages so their workers cannot fully understand what they are saying. Workers, on the other hand, develop their own slang so they can speak to one another without being understood by supervisors.

Adults regularly use words too large or too difficult for their children to understand. Children and adolescents develop a code language of their own so that adults will be left out of their conversations. An entirely new language—still a type of English, however—has been developed by C.B.ers. Only other C.B.ers fully understand what is being said, and some of them don't.

Of course all the trades and professions have their technical languages. While most legal contracts could be written in easily understandable English, lawyers resist changing the language. If everyone could understand legal documents, lawyers would lose some of their prestige and value. The same is true in medicine, ministry, and other professions.

The magazine article placed the blame for our inability to communicate on exactly the same problem that scattered the builders of Babel. The self-centered human ego, concentrating on its own desires, loses its ability to communicate (share) with others. The language has been confused.

But confusion is not God's real desire for men. His ultimate goal is once again to unite His linguistically torn creation.

> For he has made known to us in all wisdom and insight the mystery of his will, according to his purpose which he set forth in Christ as a plan for the fulness of time, *to unite all things in him*, things in heaven and things on earth (Ephesians 1:9, 10).

Disunity is not God's desire, but unity. That unity is possible through Jesus Christ. In order to communicate the love of God through Christ to all of us, God has chosen the universal language of the heart, the language of love. We may not be able to understand each other's spoken language, but we can all understand what God has said to us in the birth of a baby or a death on a cross. We can comprehend the death, burial, and resurrection pictured in Christian baptism, and the meaning of the bread and wine in the communion meal. We know how to read the empty grave.

Through Christ's language of love, the scattered peoples of the earth are again discovering their oneness. "There is one body and one Spirit, just as you were called to the one hope that belongs to your call, one Lord, one faith, one baptism, one God and Father of us all, who is above all and through all and in all" (Ephesians 4:4-6).

In Babel God scattered the proud.

In Christ He gathers the humble.

Notes

[1]Philip Lesly, "How We Discommunicate." *Passages*, February 1976, pp. 17, 18.

When God Chooses Someone

Genesis 12:1-9

In July of 1965 I resigned my ministry in Oregon to move to Tennessee. For the text of my resignation sermon I selected the record of Abram's call. Although it may have seemed a bit presumptuous to compare myself with Abram, I did feel that I had been called from my own land and people to a strange and distant place that God would show me. As I meditated on this text, with part of me desiring to make the long journey and another part resisting, I wondered what would have happened if Abram had said no to God's call. That certainly would have been the easier choice. He could have remained with his family and friends (but then I remembered the words of Jesus, "He who loves father or mother more than me is not worthy of me"). Abram must have been tempted to stay at home.

I could not fully imagine what would have happened if Abram had remained in Ur or Haran, but one thing I knew for certain. He would have missed one of the greatest adventures of history. I didn't know exactly what would happen to me either if I were to say no to

Tennessee, but I knew that I didn't want to miss whatever adventure God had in store for me. So I went like Abram to a far country.

In His call to Abram, *God announces a new day*. This is a feature of the good news that God is preparing for mankind, news that will reach its fullest expression in Christ. The history of mankind so far has been a disappointment to God. Like the blind leading the blind, men have chosen to wallow in wickedness rather than walk as friends of God. God has dealt with them harshly. He has had no other choice.

But now God seizes the initiative and announces a new nation, a special people, holy to himself, to be blessed by Him and to be a blessing to others. "Let the emphasis be upon blessing," God says. "We have had enough of curses. Abram, you will father a great nation (not numerically or geographically great, but great in the new hope you offer to all the world). Abram, I will bless you, and I will make your name great (as opposed to the citizens of an earlier era at Babel, who tried to make their name great apart from me). You will be a blessing, and through your descendants will all the families of the earth bless themselves."

In these words God announces one of His greatest themes, a theme that Christ will echo centuries later. God's concern is not only that Abram love Him and that He love Abram, but He wants Abram so to love Him that Abram will be a blessing to his neighbors. Jesus restated God's desire: "You shall love the Lord your God with all your heart, and with all your soul, and with all your mind . . . and . . . your neighbor as yourself" (Matthew 22:37-39). When men and women live in this kind of love, that will indeed be a new day.

In order to usher in the new day, *God selects a special man*.

Special may be a little strong here. The Bible doesn't indicate that Abram has been special before

God selects him. It is the selecting that makes him special. But if we want to lift up a characteristic that makes Abram God's choice, it is found in the fourth verse: obedience. Paul rightly emphasizes Abram's faith (Galatians 3:6-9) but it is faith that produces obedience (Hebrews 11:8), and faith is completed, matured, in obedience (James 2:22). Through faith Abram is able to obey the voice of God. That is his virtue.

Otherwise he certainly is not a perfect man. Just a few verses later in the twelfth chapter we see that he lies to protect his ow skin (verses 10-13). That is not perfection. But as the Bible makes clear, when God has a special task for a man to do, He often chooses a flawed personality to do His bidding. Consider Moses, with his stammering tongue and uncontrollable temper; or David, capable of so lusting after another man's wife that he will commit murder; or Solomon, wise in so many things yet surprisingly foolish; or Paul, completely dedicated to the will of God but not an easy personality to like; or Peter, impulsive and sometimes unreliable.

Why does God select such men to do His work? The answer seems to be that in each case, in spite of his obvious weaknesses, the man is obedient to the voice of God.

With obedience, then, Abram follows God's instruction and sets out, not knowing his ultimate destination. We learn more about him as we follow his journey.

He is open to adventure. This willingness to risk one's security for God is obviously a key to knowing God's will. The philosopher Alfred North Whitehead has said that "Adventure or Decadence are the only choices offered to mankind." God's way is the way of adventure. Those who choose security and comfort can never know the full will of God.

Abraham is optimistic. Although faced with more than his share of heartaches and disappointments, Abram is not defeated by discouragement. Wanting to obey the will of God, he does not fear the future but faces it expectantly. He has the very special ability, seemingly granted to only a few, to look beyond today and wait for his reward in God's good time. He dies before the fulfillment of the promise, but he dies still trusting in God's timing.

That is Abram.

But we would not be reading this passage with other than historical interest unless we felt that the call to Abram has something personally to do with us. We sense that God is still calling men and women to be a blessing to others.

How shall we respond to this call of God? Each of us must honestly answer three questions.

The first question: *Do I really want to do God's will?* Or is it more important for me to remain in my country with my kindred and father's house? That is, what do I really want most of all—luxury, comfort, solitude, friends, family, self-indulgence?

It is quite easy for us to believe we are serving God in our everyday routines, until we hear the voice of God breaking through our complacency and asking us to step out on faith, to do what we've never done before, to cut our ties with everything that makes us secure. Then we must ask, Do I really want to do God's will?

The second question naturally follows: *Do I care about others?* That is, do I want to be a blessing? If I care about others, how many do I care about? My family? My friends? My nation? All God's children?

If I do, then everything that happens in my life begins to take on new meaning. Even failures can be seen as ways by which I can now serve the Lord. Keith Miller testifies in his *Habitation of Dragons* of his growing realization that his decision to become a blessing to others was affecting him in every way, including his failures. When he first became a Christian, he said he still had a pattern of indecision and fear about his future. He felt personally inadequate, in spite of his outward decisiveness. Several years later he went through a series of job changes, so that within a period of less than five years he held five different jobs. In every case he felt the change to be definitely in line with God's will. He was willing to risk failure for the sake of service to God. He was learning that for a Christian nothing is wasted in this life. His bad decisions, his vocational changes, his personal failures can all be used to be a blessing to others. Even when he later broke his back and thought he was going to be paralyzed from the neck down, and his parents were ravaged by sickness and accident, and he was turned down on a promotion, these severe disappointments "provided the only doorways I now have into the hearts and lives of struggling men and women."[1] Because he wanted to be a blessing to others, nothing, even the worst blows that life could deal him, was wasted.

The question is, How can what happens to me be used for others? How can my venturing to a far country be used as a blessing? Since I know that the will of God for me is to be a person for others, how can who I am and what has happened to me be used to bless them?

The third major question: *Am I willing to be adventurous?* The New Testament exhorts us to be doers of the word and not hearers only. Abram's was not a speculative faith but a faith of action. The King James Version says with its simple eloquence, "And they went forth to go into the land of Canaan; and into the land of Canaan they came." Abram heard, he obeyed, and he completed his adventure.

It is one thing to say, "I want to do God's will." It is another thing to begin the journey.

One of the good members of our congregation wrote me a long and thoughtful letter about his search for God's will in his life. He comes to the end of the letter with this ringing assertion: "I'm going to make a statement. I'm willing to go anywhere, do anything, and say anything if it is the will of God. . . . Now I guess I will wait to see what happens. But it will be an active and not passive waiting." He has discovered the essence of faith. It is an active and not passive waiting. It is beginning the journey.

That's why I did not feel presumptuous when comparing myself with Abram at the time I resigned my Oregon ministry to go to Tennessee. Though Abram's call was far more significant than mine, nonetheless I did feel—and still do feel—that God was calling me to an adventure. Had I remained in Oregon, I still could have served the Lord. But oh the excitement my wife and I would have missed! We risked our security and found blessings beyond anything we could have imagined. In turn, we have been of more help to others than would have been possible had we turned our back on His call.

We know many contemporary Abrams. In our congregation are the Smiths, who prayed one day that the Lord would send missionaries to Ethiopia—and He answered their prayer, and they went. We have the Calverts, who feel a deep burden for England. They have prayed for God to send ministers to work with the churches in England. God is doing so, and the Calverts are preparing to go. We have friends all over the world who prayed and heard and went. We have others who have never left their geographical setting, but whom God has called to serve in risk-taking ways. They have heard, and have taken the risks, and have been blessings.

The secret of their courage is trust in God. In Britain during World War II, land mines were sometimes dropped by Germany. These long cylinders of steel attached to huge parachutes were treacherously dangerous. After a severe raid one night a warden saw a mine hanging from a steel girder and swaying in the breeze at daybreak. He sent for a demolition squad. When the men arrived, a thirty-foot ladder was placed against the girder and the young lieutenant ordered his men away and climbed up to the deadly mine. He examined it carefully, then took a wrench and slowly and carefully began to remove the deadly fuse. Finally he lowered the now harmless land mine to the ground.

One of his friends who had been watching the operation congratulated him and confessed that he could not do that kind of thing without being afraid.

"You are mistaken," the officer replied. "Every time I am called to one of these jobs, I am afraid, but I master my fears. I must, because if my hand trembled on the wrench, that moment would probably be my last."

"Would you mind telling me how you master your fears?" he was asked.

He hesitated a moment, then replied, "Well, it goes back to my childhood in Scotland. I've never forgotten a Bible verse my mother taught me: 'Yea, though I walk through the valley of the shadow of death, I will fear no evil: for thou art with me' (Psalm 23:4). I have been down in that valley many times, but on such occasions I'm able to master my fears, for I believe God is with me and nothing else really matters."[2]

If God is with us, we can be adventurous—for nothing else matters.

Notes

[1]Waco, Texas: Word Books, p. 16, 17.
[2]John Sutherland Bonnell, *No Escape From Life*. New York: Harper and Row, 1958, pp. 42, 43.

Faith
Under
the Knife

Genesis 22:1-18; James 2:17-26

I'm somewhat hesitant to tell you my first reaction to Abraham's journey to sacrifice Isaac. I couldn't do it, I found myself saying. I have three children, and I couldn't give up one of them. I'm afraid I must be like a preacher who was called to give a special sermon at a university chapel service. His assigned subject was missionary work. In his message he eloquently appealed to the young people to take up the cross of Christ and go as missionaries. "Who will go?" he pleaded. "Who will take the message of Christ to the steaming, disease-ridden jungles of Africa? Who will go to save those dying in heathen darkness?" As he paused a girl in the front row spoke out, "I'll go, I'll go, Father." Instinctively the preacher responded "Oh no! Not you!"

He was not the only preacher to call for the ultimate sacrifice from others but to fight against giving up one of his own children.

It is easier for me to understand that preacher than to understand Abraham. Here he rises high above us, assuming heroic dimensions. We hesitate to ask, "Can I imitate him?" We simply express our astonishment. We sense that it must have been a very black night in Abraham's soul when he heard the voice of the Lord.

But perhaps I'm overlooking something that Abraham did not forget. Before this demand, he had received many promises from his God:

When God first called Abraham He promised to make of him a great nation (Genesis 12:1-3).

After Abraham and Lot had divided up the land, the voice of the Lord came to Abraham, saying, "Lift up your eyes, and look from the place where you are, northward and southward and eastward and westward; for all the land which you see I will give to you and to your descendants for ever. I will make your descendants as the dust of the earth . . ." (Genesis 13:14-16).

When in one of his moments of discouragement Abraham complained to the Lord, saying, "Behold, thou hast given me no offspring; and a slave born in my house will be my heir," the promise of the Lord came once again: "This man shall not be your heir; your own son shall be your heir" (Genesis 15:3-6).

Then the best word of all, "Sarah your wife shall bear you a son, and you shall call his name Isaac. I will establish my covenant with him as an everlasting covenant for his descendants after him" (Genesis 17:19).

God had promised and God had delivered. Abraham had a son whose name was Isaac.

But now comes a new word from the Lord and in this word is no sound of comfort, no promise, no reminder of a covenant. Just a stark command: "Take your son, your only son Isaac, whom you love . . ." So Abraham once again starts out on a journey, this one the hardest journey of all. He must have seemed to his family a crazy man, crazier even than Noah building his boat on dry land.

Or maybe he didn't. For the Canaanite people around Abraham were accustomed to offer human sacrifices to appease their angry gods. Such sacrifices are noted in the Bible (see Micah 6:6-8 and 2 Kings 3:27). But Abraham had said his God was different. Now he was behaving as if his God were like the gods of the Canaanites. (Is it possible that God is calling him to offer his son upon the sacrificial altar in order to stop him, to prove himself different from the other gods? Could that thought have been in Abraham's mind as he journeyed to Moriah? It's possible, though not stated in the record.)

It is intriguing to speculate about God's motives in this surprising command, but such speculation is not very helpful for us. What is important is its challenge to our complacency. It demands a rethinking of our faith in God. To grasp fully what is happening to Abraham in these verses is to learn anew three simple lessons of faith.

The first lesson: *to hear is to obey.*

The Hebrew word for *obey* is simply *hear*. When one has heard the word of God, he does what God commands. My father, who might be surprised to be compared to the ancient Hebrews, nonetheless had the same understanding of hearing and obeying. He would frequently follow his instructions to his children with a word he borrowed and transformed from the Spanish: "Savvy?" There was no question about it. If I understood what he was saying, I would do it! (I have been trying to teach my own children the relationship between hearing and obeying, but I do not seem to be quite as good an instructor as my father was.) Abraham had no doubt that God had spoken to him. Having heard, he had no choice but to obey.

So Abraham arose. With heaviness of heart, almost crazy with grief, fighting every step of the way to keep from turning back, he went toward Moriah. What was in his heart? Doubt as to whether he had really heard, bitterness because of the almost unbearably harsh demand, utter bewilderment because the God who had given was now taking away? What we know is that he had heard— and oh, how he must have wished he had not heard—the word of God. He had no choice but to obey. He needed no instruction to be a doer of the word and not a hearer only. To hear was to do. For Abraham believed in God.

The second lesson is simply a restatement of the first: *to believe is to do.* This is the point that James is making in his letter: "So faith by itself, if it has no works, is dead." Because Abraham believed God, James insists, he did what God wanted and was therefore justified.

How frequently people say, "I believe in God, *but* . . ." I'm frequently tempted to ask such people, "What is the evidence that you believe? Does your family have any reason to think you pay God any more than lip service? Can your neighbors or your fellow employees tell that you believe in God?" I discount a person's protest that he believes unless I can see through his works that he does.

I frequently tell my congregation, "If you want me to know what you really believe, let me see your check book. After I go through your check stubs and find out what you spend money for, then I will know what you believe." That's simply an updated way of saying, "So faith apart from works is dead."

To believe is to do.

God: "Abraham, do you really believe in me?"
Abraham: "Yes, Lord, you know I believe."
God: "Abraham, how much do you believe in me?"
Abraham: "With all my heart I believe in you, Lord."
God: "Abraham, do you believe I'll keep all the promises I have made to you?"

Abraham: "Yes, Lord, you know I believe you will keep the promises."

God: "Then Abraham, take your son, your only son . . . and give him back to me."

Abraham is trapped. He has said he believes. Now the test.

In Martin Luther's famous preface to his commentary on Romans, he defines faith as "a living, well-founded confidence in the grace of God, perfectly certain that it would die a thousand times rather than surrender its conviction. Such confidence and personal knowledge of divine grace makes its possessor joyful, bold, and full of warm affection toward God and all created things . . ." When he wrote those words Luther could not have been thinking of Abraham on the road to Moriah. On that trip Abraham certainly was anything but joyful. Could he have felt warm affection toward God as he prepared to take the life of his only son—under God's orders? Does faith always make one joyful and affectionate? I don't think so, and neither did Luther. Elsewhere he defines faith as "a great art and doctrine, which no saint has learned and fathomed fully unless he has found himself in despair, in the anguish of death, or in extreme peril." That was Abraham's experience. He found the depths of his faith in the depths of his anguish.

But he knew, as we know, that to believe is to do.

This has sounded too negative; for there is another side of faith, and on that side Abraham is relying.

It is the third lesson: *to believe God is to trust Him.* God keeps His promises. He had promised Isaac and He had delivered. Now Abraham must trust God's promise regarding Isaac's descendants, even as he prepares to take Isaac's life.

The writer of Hebrews offers an explanation for Abraham's bold act:

By faith Abraham, when he was tested, offered up Isaac, and he who had received the promises was ready to offer up his only son, of whom it was said, "Through Isaac shall your descendants be named." He considered that *God was able to raise men even from the dead*; hence, figuratively speaking, he did receive him back (Hebrews 11:17-19).

Abraham's God is the God of the living and the dead. He keeps His promises. He is the God who gives and the God who takes and the God who gives back. So trusting God, Abraham could keep his appointment at Moriah. To Abraham, faith is a surrender in trust of one's heart, soul, mind, body, and strength to God.

Such faith enabled Abraham to obey God, even in the presence of the horrified look in Sarah's face, the fear in his servant's eyes, the anguish in his own heart, and the doubt in his mind that rises up to challenge every act of faith. In spite of everything, Abraham trusted.

And his trust was not in vain. Isaac was spared.

Centuries later, another Son was offered in sacrifice. But with a difference. That Son died. His death was terrible, His anguish excruciating. He cried out, "My God, my God, why have you forsaken me?" He had trusted His Heavenly Father, and His Father had allowed Him to be slain.

But His trust was not in vain. The Lord of the living and the dead allowed Him to be killed, to be buried, to be sealed up. But He did not allow death to be victorious. Through Christ's resurrection God proved himself to be the promise-keeping God in whom all human beings can trust their lives, knowing that He is able to take them even through death to himself.

To believe God is to trust Him, even under the knife.

Working
for a Life

Genesis 26:12-25

In chapter eight we studied one of the most dramatic moments in Genesis. When God called Abraham to lead his son Isaac to Mount Moriah and offer him there as a sacrifice, He sternly tested the patriarch's faith. Abraham's experience still grips the imagination of every believer.

Because Genesis 22 tells such a remarkable story, however, it is imperative that we turn quickly to Genesis 26. I have selected it arbitrarily, for there are many other chapters that could as effectively remind us that the life of faith is seldom as dramatic as Abraham's trial. This is a commonplace Scripture. It reports that Isaac, whose life was spared on Mount Moriah, grew to be a man who lived a rather ordinary life. He sowed and reaped and became wealthy, he watched over his flocks and herds and household, he had struggles with unsympathetic neighbors, he observed the proper religious rituals, and he was blessed by the God of Abraham. Isaac's life does not seem ever to have had the luster of his father's before him.

In other words, Isaac seems to be a lot more like us. If his life seems rather uneventful, so does ours. Yet Isaac was called of God as surely as his father. His call, like ours, seems to have been to an ordinary life. He worked hard and prospered, he fathered sons who pleased and disappointed him, he loved a wife who served and manipulated him. Through it all, God blessed him.

In all his labors, Isaac served God and knew that he was called of Him, even if only to work. Isaac had no doubt that he was working for a life, a life with God.

In this chapter let's consider the meaning of a believer's work—ordinary, everyday, routine, even dull work.

In the beginning work and life were undivided. When God created Adam, he placed him in the garden to till it and keep it (Genesis 2:15). Even before Eve came into being, God called her a helper of man (2:18). She too was identified with her work.

The Bible places no stigma on work. The activity of God himself is called work:

O Lord, how manifold are thy *works*!
In wisdom hast thou made them all;
   the earth is full of thy creatures.

—Psalm 104:24

Of His divine mission Jesus said, "I glorified thee on earth, having accomplished *the work* which thou gavest me to do" (John 17:4).

The apostle Paul exhorted Christians "to aspire to live quietly, to mind your own affairs, and *to work with your hands*, as we charged you; so that you may command the respect of outsiders, and be dependent on nobody" (1 Thessalonians 4:11, 12).

The Scriptures teach that God's call is not to an honored position, but to a good work. This stands in bold contrast with other ancient cultures. The Hebrews were unlike the ancient Greeks, whose intellectuals disdained to get their hands dirty and thought of common labor as beneath their dignity. They would have scoffed at Genesis' commendation of the working life.

Some of us scoff with them. Accuse the average laborer or professional of enjoying his work and he'll vehemently deny it. He is only working because he has to, he protests. He probably thinks the Bible's praise of work quite unrealistic. To him, the best description of work is *drudgery*.

What makes it so unsatisfying to so many?

The answer is found in Genesis 3:17-19. When Adam and Eve rebelled against God and received His discipline, God cursed the ground and promised toil, sweat, thorns, and thistles in place of the pleasures of tilling Eden's soil. Sin did not make labor necessary, but obviously made it less rewarding. When the work was no longer for God, but for survival, it turned into hard labor.

As I was preparing this study, I reviewed my own work history. I felt the call of God to preach while I was in high school. Because our family had limited means, I knew I would have to work my way through college, taking whatever job I could get. In the fourteen years of my college and university career, I worked as a janitor, a ditchdigger, a fisherman, a grocer, a house painter, an assistant landscape gardener, a choir director, a schoolteacher, an apartment-house manager, and a garbage man. This review of my employment record made me realize that when God called me to preach He was also calling me to work. Many of those jobs would have seemed drudgery except that they were all a part of my response to the call of God. I could now go back to any one of them without loss of self respect, so long as my labor and my service were related. Work fell from grace when men fell from God, but when one is working for God and open to His bidding, any task takes on new meaning and dignity. One needs never to feel embarrassed when doing whatever God gives him to do.

In the beginning, then, a man's work and his life were one and good. When man rebelled and fell from God, his work fell with him. When any person rises to God, his work is likewise elevated.

Let's look at the call of God to Abraham. God wanted Abraham to go from his country, kindred, and father's house to a new land. This was a call to live by faith and by work. Seldom did God ask Abraham to prepare to do the dramatic (as in Genesis 22). Most of his life was quite ordinary. He was to oversee his many possessions, take care of his kinfolk, observe the normal acts of piety and worship, intercede in domestic squabbles, barter for land, manage his finances, and in other unspectacular ways live for God. In this respect, Abraham was no different from Isaac, nor from Noah, whose response in faith was hard work. When God called me to preach, he also called me to be a janitor, a ditchdigger, a fisherman, a grocer, a house painter, etc. And when He called you to live for Him, He assumed that you would work uneventfully, but that through your ordinary tasks you would praise and serve Him.

Some people are trapped in unpromising jobs that yield few opportunities to serve God. So they live double lives. They earn their living at the plant, but center their life in the church. They sing in the choir, teach Sunday school, serve on the board, participate in the visitation program, or find some other way to work for God. This double life enables them to endure their frustrations on the job while receiving joy and satisfaction in their true vocation, which is serving God.

I admire such people. I often think that theology is developed less in the quiet study of scholars than in the sweat and heat of day-by-day work, where the dictates of God meet the demands of the job. God's real theologians are not the professors of theology, but the doers of it—on the job and in the church.

L. P. Jacks told of an old Irish unskilled laborer who worked in railway construction long before the days of power machinery. His tool was a shovel, a spade that shone like stainless steel when he cleaned it up at night. When he was asked what he would say for himself when he died and met his Maker, he responded, "I think I'll just show him my spade."

Jacks, who authored many books and wrote his manuscripts out in longhand, always wore an old tweed jacket. "If it comes to that," he said, "I think I'll show God the cuffs of my jacket."[1]

I wonder what I'll show.

Remember James? "Show me your faith apart from your works, and I by my works will show you my faith. . . . You see that a man is justified by works and not by faith alone. . . . For as the body apart from the spirit is dead, so faith apart from works is dead" (2:18, 24, 26).

The call of God, then, is a call to work. In answering that call, one discovers the joy of work in God.

Consider the joy of Joseph, Isaac's grandson (Genesis 37—48). Spoiled by his father and despised by his older brothers, Joseph was sold into slavery and transported to Egypt. But having the God-given gift of interpreting dreams, Joseph eventually rose to become second in command to the Pharaoh. When he explained the famine foretold in the Pharaoh's dream, Joseph was appointed virtual dictator of the land so that he could prepare during the seven years of good harvest for the coming seven years of famine.

When the famine became severe, his brothers made their journey from their father's house to Egypt in search of food. When Joseph finally disclosed his true identity to them, they were horrified and frightened.

They knew what they deserved from him. But he reassured them:

> And not do not be distressed, or angry with yourselves, because you sold me here; for *God sent me before you to preserve life*. For the famine has been in the land these two years; and there are yet five years in which there will be neither plowing nor harvest. And *God sent me before you to preserve for you a remnant on earth, and to keep alive for you many survivors. So it was not you who sent me here, but God* (Genesis 45:5-8).

What joy that speech must have given Joseph! "God sent me before you to save life." Joseph accepted his ability to interpret dreams as a gift from God, and in the same way he regarded his opportunity to assist Egypt in preparing for the famine. God then gave him the further joy of saving his own family from starvation. He experienced what Christ would later teach, that "it is more blessed to give than to receive" (Acts 20:35).

Joseph's experience leads us to ask ourselves at least three questions:

First, what work am I prepared to do for God? He gave Joseph the gift of interpretation, and Joseph used that gift for God. How has God prepared me—what gift has He given me—to work for Him?

Second, where is God leading me to serve? He led Joseph to Egypt. Is it possible that He has led me to the job I am currently holding, that I may serve Him through that job? Is this position a step toward another in which I may serve Him even more fully?

Third, am I using God's gift for the work He has given me? (Or to ask it another way, Who is benefiting from my work?)

Think about these two Christians. The first, Bill J., has the reputation of being a deeply religious person. He reads many books of devotion and Bible study; he subscribes to several Christian magazines, especially those dealing with faith healing. On his shelves are books on positive thinking. But Bill doesn't work for a living. He complains of a chronic illness, though the doctors find little evidence of it. He is supported by his wife, who seldom complains of the load that she has to carry. Bill frequently testifies about the saving grace of God who has helped him so much in spite of his severe physical handicaps. He says he has faith. He does not feel called to work.

But then consider Sue W. She thinks of herself as a Biblical illiterate, although she does try to study whenever she can find a little time. She is too timid to stand before a group to speak about her faith, but she will take any job others consider themselves too good to do. She loves her family and works long hours for them and still finds it possible to carry in food for her sick neighbors. She works in the nursery at her church. She would not ever think of herself as a woman of great faith, although she has heard the call of God to work, and in her work she has found joy.

Would you say Bill or Sue has a clearer insight into the relation of faith to work?

In my life there have been no dramatic moments of faith like that of Abraham on Mount Moriah. My life has been much more like Isaac's: sowing and reaping, managing my possessions, looking after my family, and working for a living. But I refuse to think that I just work for a living. I work for a life, a life with God.

Don't you feel the same about your work?

Notes
[1]Quoted in William Barclay, *Ethics in a Permissive Society*. New York: Harper and Row, © 1971, p. 96.

Hunting for a Wife

Genesis 24:1-9; 28:1-5

During most of these Genesis studies we have felt quite at home. The major themes we have discovered have proved that the problems and opportunities confronting ancient people were similar to our own. But the subject of marriage discloses the distance between Genesis and the twentieth century, because some of the marriage customs of old differ drastically from ours. When we read that Abraham sends his servant to select a wife for Isaac (chapter 24) and later learn that Isaac in turn forbids his son to marry a Canaanite woman but sends him back to his mother's people to find a wife (chapter 28), we feel ourselves suddenly in a very strange world.

In Genesis there are some customs that we may or may not like. To begin with the first major difference, marriage was arranged *on behalf of* the groom and bride, *not by* them. It was a father's responsibility to select a mate for the son or daughter; young men and young women did not take care of that matter themselves.

Since we "moderns" believe in "falling in love" and are convinced that romantic passion is a requirement for the love that leads to marriage, we refuse to submit to an arranged marriage.

(I remember that my parents had a girl picked out for me. Oh, boy! She was—and is—a fine person. But both of us agree that it would have been less than an ideal match! So you understand that I'm not exactly advocating arranged marriages, although now that I have some children approaching marriageable age, I think maybe it's not a bad idea.)

We believe in romantic love, but we will have to admit that something has gone wrong with many modern marriages. Perhaps our romantic illusions have a little bit to do with our marital failures. Is there some truth in what George Bernard Shaw says?

When two people are under the influence of the most violent, most insane, most delusive, and most transient of passions, they are required to swear that they will remain in that excited, abnormal, and exhausting condition continuously until death do them part.

There is certainly a contradiction between our stated reasons for marrying and our real reasons for staying married. We pledge our vows "in love." Practically, however, we stay together because of a combination of factors: common social and economic background, influence of our parents' values and stability, common responsibilities, and the conviction that marriage is permanent and worth working to maintain.

When we talk of falling in love we're not thinking of these practical matters. We're experiencing instead some kind of feeling, a warm but temporary glow. When the passion is gone the marriage is threatened.

I'm very much concerned about this. Frankly, my record isn't very good. Too many of the couples that I have married are no longer together.

Yet as I think back over the counselling sessions I held with the couples before the weddings, I recall vividly that all of them said to me that they wanted to get married because "we're so much in love." Maybe that term "in love" is what is getting us into trouble. Certainly we are not using it in the Biblical sense. Love in the Bible is not something we can fall into and out of. "Love never ends," the Bible says. Infatuation or passion is not the same as love.

When the popular television hero5ine Rhoda Morgenstern married in front of millions of TV viewers, she and her groom vowed to be true and faithful to each other as long as they both should love. What kind of pledge is that? As long as I feel good about you, I'll stay with you. What happened to "in sickness and health," or "for richer or for poorer," or "for better or for worse"? Is it any wonder that Rhoda's marriage ended in divorce?

If love is not an act of will, an act of commitment, I don't know from a Biblical point of view what it is. Perhaps until we know what love really is we should return to the arranged marriage and learn that love is something you grow into. It has to do with making a pledge and meaning it and keeping it.

That's the first lesson from Genesis: *Marriage is arranged.* Abraham and Isaac assume responsibility for their sons, trusting God to lead them.

The Lord, the God of heaven, who took me from my father's house and from the land of my birth, and who spoke to me and swore to me, 'To your descendants I will give this land,' he will send his angel before you, and you shall take a wife for my son from there (Genesis 24:7).

Here is the second lesson from Genesis: *Marriage is from one's own kind.* An important principle yet!

Abraham is sending for a wife for his son from among his own people. Her background will be his background, her people his people. They will understand one another and be of common faith. Isaac sends Jacob to his mother's relatives for the same reason.

I'm going to sound very old-fashioned now, but I realize I have not said enough against mixed marriages in my ministry. When two people decide they want to get married, among the first questions I always ask them is "Tell me about your religion, your faith." It is your faith that determines how you spend your money, who your friends are, what you do for recreation, what your career will be, how you'll raise your children. Everything is involved in your faith. So when two people of dissimilar faith decide to marry, they are asking for trouble.

Abraham and Isaac after him knew that they had been called of God, and they wanted their descendants to remain special to Him. The only way they could protect that special relationship was to be certain that the faith was not adulterated through marriage. The fathers wanted to pass to their descendants faith in the true God. They wanted them not to be like everyone else, but unique.

This principle makes for good marriages. Marriage ought to be from one's own kind.

In addition to questions about faith we must raise some other ones. Do you have similar education? (We know that if there is a big gap between the spouses' levels of education there may very well be a problem in the relationship.)

How do your parents get along? What kind of a home did you grow up in? (They will tend to reproduce what they saw in their parent's homes, so if their homes were quite different they are going to have some terrible tensions.)

Similar questions must be asked about their social habits and about their economic levels.

We like the story in which Cinderella marries the prince—but it is just a fairy story. Cinderellas and princes almost never live happily ever after. There are too many differences.

The third lesson from Genesis is that *marriage is for children* (24:7; 28:3). One of the primary goals, of course, was to perpetuate the people. It was imperative to have many children because of the high infant mortality rate, the many wars, the epidemics.

You will recall how desperately Abraham and Sarah yearned for a son, with an impatience that prompted Sarah to offer her handmaiden Hagar to Abraham in order to insure an heir for him (Genesis 16). Later Jacob's favorite wife Rachel suffered anguish because of her barren condition (30:1). In each of these families, children were regarded as a blessing from God. They received them with thanksgiving and devoted themselves to teaching them thoroughly about the God of their special covenant (Deuteronomy 6).

There is no longer the urgency about bearing children that we note in Genesis. Many of the couples I marry have decided to have none or at most one or two. With the reduced mortality rate and the increased living standard we now enjoy, children are not always viewed as a blessing from God, and the drive to perpetuate a family name or a special relationship with God is noticeably absent.

For us parents, however, children remain very much a blessing. I could list many of the joys they introduce into a home, but let me just mention one: they require us to be better than we would be without them. I cannot count the number of times I have had to behave better than I have wanted to, just because the children were around. It is true that they sometimes bring out the worst in me, but on balance they have improved my behavior.

It is good that there is no longer a stigma against being childless, a stigma that both Sarah and Rachel suffered so keenly. But there is a sense in which childless couples are deprived. They have no little ones dependent on them, requiring sacrifices from them, demanding maturity and responsibility and good examples. My counsel to the childless is to "borrow" some children or dependent adults to whom they can give themselves and their means. The world is full of persons in need. They are just waiting for someone to love them.

No marriage can be complete with just a husband and a wife living for each other. There must be others with whom the partners can share.

The fourth lesson on marriage from Genesis is sometimes overlooked: *marriage is for pleasure.* As you read through the Old Testament passages you recognize that there was something beautiful in the relationship between Abraham and Sarah, for example, or Jacob and Rachel. (Now this can get complicated because I'm leaving out a few of the wives. It was a polygamous society, and I'm not recommending that we return to it. I can't afford it, and there are too many problems attached to it!)

The old book of Common Prayer says that marriage was given by God for three reasons. The first was procreation of children, the second was so that we might avoid fornication, and the third was for mutual society, help, and comfort. It's this third reason that I'm talking about now.

Marriage is for pleasure. Let the home be filled with laughter and acceptance and adventure and sexual gratification; and best of all, let it be filled with friendship between husband and wife.

Let them be like the husband and wife at the airport saying goodbye to their last child. She was boarding a plane to go off to college, and her mother began to cry. "Now all I have left is you," she said to her husband. He was an understanding man, so he put his arm around her and reassured her: "Well, I'm all you had to begin with." That's how it ought to be. It's a traumatic time when the last child leaves home, but in a mutually gratifying marriage, pleasure continues.

There is one more lesson from Genesis that I ought to mention, and that is that *marriage is for keeps*. There is no mention here of divorce. In the New Testament, Jesus says that it was allowed because of the hardness of our hearts (Matthew 19:8). It's quite evident that divorce is not in God's plan. His design is that a man and a woman live together and help one another until death.

We know that's true. The question is, What are we going to do about this standard in our society?

We could go to either of two extremes, both of them wrong, I think. The one extreme is a legalistic one that calls divorce a sin and makes no place in the church for the divorced and closes all leadership positions to all divorced persons. You can make a strong case for this position. I know many churches that do. But I believe them to be violating the spirit of Christ.

You then can go to the other extreme, pointing to the prevalence of divorce and accepting it as a fact of life, saying nothing against it. But that would be to disregard the clear teaching of the Scriptures. The Bible states unmistakably that God desires for the marriage vows to be permanent.

What then shall we do? We must choose the much more difficult pathway between those extremes. We must admit that the Scriptures call divorce a sin. But we must insist that the Scriptures do not make divorce the unpardonable sin.

And if I sense the spirit of the Scriptures correctly, Jesus came that all who sin and fall short of the glory of God may receive forgiveness of their sins and a new chance. We can abuse His grace, of course. But isn't it possible for us to clasp each other as fellow sinners—you with your sins, me with mine—and all ask God's forgiveness? Can't we promise to help each other to grow in grace and Christlikeness? Shouldn't we hold the doors of the church open for sinners of all kinds?

I do not want to encourage promiscuousness. I disapprove of it. But I do want to encourage redemption. So I pledge myself to do everything I can to help every marriage in our church survive, and not only to survive but to flourish, and not only to flourish but to be pleasurable. I wish for all people marriage like that of my grandparents, who loved each other during sixty-four years together. Their marriage was for keeps.

It is a long way from the arranged, unbreakable marriages of the ancient Hebrews to the casual love-matches of our culture. We may not want to return to a system in which parents take charge of matchmaking—although current divorce statistics cannot argue persuasively for the superiority of our romantic approach—but a careful study of Biblical marriages from Genesis through the New Testament can at least stimulate critical thinking about the state of matrimony in the twentieth century. As we see marriage in Genesis,

- love is expected to grow through the years.
- husband and wife share common faith and culture.
- children are a blessing from God, requiring the best from mother and father.
- the giving of pleasure is expected.
- the promises are for keeps.

Have we really improved it in these modern times?

Trouble in the Family

Genesis 27

Even though God called Abraham and his descendants to be a special people, with a special assignment and agreement with Him, there isn't anything very unusual about their family behavior. What started with Adam and Eve continues throughout the Genesis record: there is trouble in the family.

Let's talk about the parents first. Using Genesis 27 as our text, we spot a serious problem in Isaac and Rebekah's relationship: *the lack of unity between husband and wife.* Isaac is the recognized head of the house; but Rebekah, like many wives after her, knows how to get around him. It is easier for her now that he has grown old and his eyes are dim. Whatever else may be said about Rebekah, she is a scheming, deceiving woman.

(I have often joked about my wife's ability to get what she wanted in our earlier years together. If I would refuse—and I often did—she would persist with her requests until I would become angry and say too much too loudly. Then I'd feel so repentant when she

76

cried—as she always did when I shouted—that I'd be overwhelmed with feelings of guilt, so I'd finally give her more than she requested in the first place. I share this incident with you to assure you that I know something about lack of unity in the home!)

In Isaac's home there is another problem. The parents are playing favorites. Esau is Isaac's favorite; Rebekah's is Jacob, whom she keeps close to her while Esau is out hunting. Her preference for Jacob unfortunately teaches him a behavioral pattern that he later follows in selecting a favorite, Joseph, from among his many sons.

We are concerned about Isaac and Rebekah's problems because this couple violates some essential principles of effective parenting. In place of their disunity there must be *parental unity*. Husband and wife have to agree on the fundamentals. It has been said that the best gift parents can give their children is their own real love affair. I agree. The love between husband and wife and the unity that grows out of their love give children a sense of security that enriches them for life.

Another essential, instead of the deception and dishonesty we see in Genesis 27, is *honesty*: that is, it is essential if the parents want their children to be honest. It isn't always easy to be truthful, of course, so we unwittingly teach our children to lie in little ways: by not answering the doorbell but sending the child to say the parents aren't home, or by being very sweet to somebody's face but critical behind his back. Children are alert to our deceptions. It is imperative that parents be honest.

And in their love they *must not play favorites* among the children. Psychiatrists are making fortunes doing nothing more complicated than trying to restore a sense of worth to adults who felt slighted by their parents. Parents dare not show partiality.

Now let's talk about the children. They contribute their share to the trouble in the family. We know today that the stresses children bring into a home are so strong they can split a marriage.

The narrative faults Esau for his *casual disregard for his birthright*. Earlier, as we see in chapter 25, Esau exchanges his special privilege and responsibility as the firstborn son for a bowl of pottage. Yes, he was hot and tired and hungry; that we can understand. But to have so little regard for his name and role in the family marks Esau as one of the Bible's less honorable personalities. Unfortunately he is not the only one in history who has shirked his family duties. Let's not follow his example.

Another problem in this family is *sibling rivalry*. The two brothers are rivals, encouraged in their competition by their parents. Jacob and Esau are like kids fighting in the backyard, each determined that the other will not be the favored one. I have observed bitterness between very young children and very old ones. In one congregation I served, two brothers in their seventies refused to have anything to do with each other because of a supposed slight. I could never tell which brother was really at fault. I suspect that this rivalry started early in their childhood and had marked their whole lives.

Esau also *disappoints his parents in his marriage*. It is a sad moment in a parent's life when a child marries unwisely. When Esau was forty years old and should have known better, "he took to wife Judith the daughter of Beeri the Hittite, and Basemath the daughter of Elon the Hittite; and they made life bitter for Isaac and Rebekah" (Genesis 26:34, 35).

We give birth to children in hope, but hope often turns to sorrow. In ancient days a woman could achieve her true purpose in life only through childbearing. Only fathering children could guarantee a man the perpetuation of his name on earth. So woman and man alike hoped for many children. But the blessing could become a burden. "The trouble with your children," some very wise person said, "is that when they are not being a lump in the throat they are being a pain in the neck." God's children sometimes disappoint, and so do ours.

I don't know about you, but I find some encouragement in the fact that Genesis does not present perfect families for us. Had Abraham's descendants been faultless, I would be tempted to interpret the troubles in our church families—and in my own—as proof that we are not God's people. To believe that would make our disappointment turn into despair. What is encouraging about this Genesis account is the fact that through it all and in it all God remains faithful to His people. In Genesis 26:24, for example, the Lord appears to Isaac and says, "I am the God of Abraham your father; fear not, for I am with you and will bless you and multiply your descendants for my servant Abraham's sake." Throughout the Bible God speaks to Abraham's descendants and reaffirms His pledge: "I am the God of Abraham, and of Isaac, and of Jacob. As I helped their trouble-torn families, so I will help you if you will remain faithful to me."

Nowhere does the Bible promise us Christians that there will be no trouble in our families. But there is still the promise that God will not be unfaithful to those who are His.

In the light of God's faithfulness, then, what should we do? How shall we live in order to keep as much trouble as possible out of the family? A friend of mine, an experienced family counselor, says that we must teach our children three things: correct knowledge of God, correct attitudes toward God and one another, and behavior that correctly expresses the knowledge and attitudes.

Knowledge by itself is inadequate, but it is essential. The Old Testament was reverently preserved by Israel's leaders in order to hand down to subsequent generations the true knowledge of God. The vital educational role was spelled out in Deuteronomy 6, and it is the role of present-day parents.

> Hear, O Israel: The Lord our God is one Lord; and you shall love the Lord your God with all your heart, and with all your soul, and with all your might. And these words which I command you this day shall be upon your heart; and you shall teach them diligently to your children, and shall talk of them when you sit in your house, and when you walk by the way, and when you lie down, and when you rise.

For some time I have saved part of an article written by a Jewish rabbi, entitled, "Do I Have to Be Jewish?" His reasoning is gentle and modern, but he speaks in the tradition of Deuteronomy 6:

> Now you're probably thinking that we are not really giving you a choice because we send you to a religious school. There is a good reason for what we are doing. We believe in Judaism. We have a responsibility to you as parents. We have to teach you what we think is important and true to prepare you for your responsibilities toward humanity as an adult. We believe that Judaism is the best religion for you. It has been that for us. Therefore, it is our obligation to see that you study Judaism. Of course we want you to know about other religions too. You will learn about them in religious school. But Judaism is the religion that is natural for you because it is the religion of your parents and it is your religion.[1]

The rabbi is counting on the truth in Proverbs 22:6. He wants to train up his children in the way they should go.

What, then, say we Christian parents? Isn't the imparting of our religious heritage every bit as important? Don't we have an obligation to impart the knowledge of God and of Christian morality to our children? That's part of our teaching responsibility.

The second part is harder. Children need to learn correct attitudes. Knowledge is taught to our children; that we can somewhat control. But our attitudes are caught by them, even when we don't want them to be. I am often rather proud of my children when they exhibit mastery of a bit of knowledge I have passed on to them. But from time to time they embarrass me, because they have picked up some of my attitudes that I don't want them to catch. I am ashamed of those attitudes in myself. I wouldn't deliberately teach them to the children, but they have learned them anyway.

For example, I have tried to teach the children to be honest. When they are, I am pleased. But when their honesty is hissed with hostility, or shouted in anger, or calculated to hurt, then I blush. Honesty can sometimes be used in a most vicious way. It is no wonder that Paul assured the Ephesian Christians that he was trying to speak the truth to them *in love* (Ephesians 4:15). Honesty was not sufficient. Love was a necessary additive. Very often the truth spoken by well-meaning persons conveys ugliness or hostility or contempt or anger rather than knowledge.

We have to remember that Jesus' enemies were the Pharisees. They had, they believed, correct knowledge. But history has condemned them as enemies of God. Their attitude was wrong, and so their knowledge was misused.

What, then, should be our attitude as parents? Let Colossians 3:12-16 be our guide:

Put on then, as God's chosen ones,
  holy and beloved,
    compassion
     kindness
      lowliness
       meekness and
        patience,
          forbearing one another and . . .
          forgiving each other; as the
          Lord has forgiven you, so
          you also must forgive.
And above all these put on love, which binds
everything together in perfect harmony. And let
the peace of Christ rule in your hearts, to which
indeed you were called in the one body. And be
thankful. Let the word of Christ dwell in you
richly, as you teach and admonish one another
in all wisdom . . .

The way we walk, the way we talk, and the way we
deal with one another we have learned from our parents. So our children will learn from us.

  How can we break the cycle? We can't.

  How then can we improve upon what we teach?
Here's a suggestion:

Therefore be imitators of God, as beloved children. And walk in love, as Christ loved us and
gave himself up for us, a fragrant offering and
sacrifice to God (Ephesians 5:1, 2).

As our children see us imitating God, they'll be able
to pattern their behavior after the best model of all.
They were created, after all, in the image of God.

Notes

[1]Copyright 1963 Christian Century Foundation. Reprinted by permission from the February 1963 issue of *The Pulpit*, now *The Christian
Ministry*.

The Cost of Doing Right

Genesis 39

"What did I ever do to deserve this?"

Have you ever asked that question? It comes quickly to our lips during severe illness or when we have suffered financial setbacks, or—and this is sometimes hardest to take—when criticism is buffeting us about and we are being condemned for something that is not our fault.

Perhaps you have done nothing to deserve the treatment you are getting. The problem may be that you have done right in a world gone wrong. You may be suffering because in serving the Lord of Heaven you have offended the prince of this world. Maybe you were honest when dishonesty would have been to your advantage.

You may be paying the price for doing right.

That's Joseph's problem. Joseph is a *natural leader*, a successful man. The Lord causes all that he does to prosper. A mere slave, he rises dramatically till he is in charge of Potiphar's entire estate, so that Potiphar has "no concern for anything but the food" that he eats.

And as you know, Joseph later becomes the chief administrator for all of Egypt. A natural leader, we would call him.

Maybe *natural* is not the right word. When Ted Williams, baseball superstar of the 1940's and 1950's, was asked about his natural ability he quickly retorted, "There's no such thing, as a natural-born hitter. I became a good hitter because I paid the price of constant practice." It takes ability, yes, but more than ability. It takes constant hard work to achieve success in any field. Joseph's leadership arose because he combined ability with energy.

Such a man, especially when he is also intelligent and physically attractive, is often quite appealing sexually. Potiphar's wife thinks so. This experienced, powerful, glamorous woman wants Joseph. Surely Joseph must be tempted. He is a rejected and inexperienced man, a stranger in a strange land, far away from the disapproving eyes of his family. He could rationalize as one of our modern songs does, "It can't be wrong when it feels so right."

But Joseph is a *man of integrity*, and an honest man is trustworthy even when no one is looking. A man of integrity is one who is what he seems to be; his private behavior matches his public face.

"My master has no concern about anything in the house," Joseph insists. "Even his wife," he could add. He will not betray the trust of his master, even at the insistence of his master's wife.

Such integrity is rare. It is valued all the more for its scarcity. Harry Truman, explaining how as president this former Missouri haberdasher could work so harmoniously with his Secretary of State, the urbane, Harvard-educated Dean Acheson, said, "I sensed immediately that he was a man I could count on in every way. I knew that he would do what had to be done, and I knew that I could count on him to tell me the truth at all times." Truman went on to emphasize that persons in positions of authority have to be able to count on a man's word. "A liar in public life is a lot more dangerous than a full, paid-up Communist."[1]

Joseph's integrity is rooted in his conviction that to betray his master would be sin not only against him, but against God: "How then can I do this great wickedness, and sin against God?" But it is frighteningly easy to yield to temptation, even in the name of God. *Christian Life* magazine for years had an annual feature entitled "100 Largest Sunday Schools." They had to stop it. Some churches were going into bankruptcy, trying too hard to climb the ladder of success. But there was another and sadder reason. The editors discovered that some churches were cheating on their attendance figures. In the name of God!

We turn in relief from today's religious success scramblers to Joseph, who had sufficient integrity and faith to fail, in a worldly sense. Success was not everything to him. Honor before God was!

Joseph is a good example for all of us, including us ministers. Our Bible colleges and seminaries may be unwittingly guilty of infecting their students with the deadly disease of worldly success. The examples usually held before students are big names, so some seminarians become convinced that they too must become evangelists like Billy Graham, entertainers like Anita Bryant, church builders like Robert Schuller, authors like Hal Lindsay, or faith healers like Oral Roberts. Success is what matters! They are not prepared to offer even their failure to God. They have not pondered the disturbing words of Jesus, "What is exalted among men is an abomination in the sight of God" (Luke 16:15). It was He who also said, "But many that are first will be last, and the last first" (Matthew 19:30). And, "If any one would be first, he must be last of all and servant of all" (Mark 9:35).

Jesus values integrity more than what is usually called success.

Joseph anticipated Jesus' teaching. He was a man of integrity. But he paid the price. He became *a man of sorrows*. It must have grieved him to be so wrongfully condemned. He knew he looked guilty. She had his garment. She was Potiphar's wife. What was his word against hers? There was no way Joseph could establish his innocence. He had tried to do right. Now he had to pay.

I said that Joseph anticipated Jesus' teaching. In this instance he also anticipated Jesus' experience. One of the Master's titles, as you know, is *man of sorrows*.

> He was despised and rejected by men;
> a man of sorrows, and acquainted with grief;
> and as one from whom men hide their faces
> he was despised, and we esteemed him not.
> —Isaiah 53:3

Jesus warned His disciples that His fate would also be theirs:

> You will be hated by all for my name's sake (Matthew 10:22). If the world hates you, know that it has hated me before it hated you. If you were of the world, the world would love its own; but because you are not of the world, but I chose you out of the world, therefore the world hates you (John 15:18, 19).

In the darkness of the night before His death, Jesus prayed to God for those disciples:

> I have given them thy word; and the world has hated them because they are not of the world,

even as I am not of the world. I do not pray that thou shouldst take them out of the world, but that thou shouldst keep them from the evil one (John 17:14, 15).

Jesus' followers share His sorrow. They have rejected this world's values, so they can expect the world to retaliate by rejecting them. When they live for Christ, when they stand for truth and righteousness and justice, they too experience something of the anguish of the man of sorrows.

The abuse that came to Joseph as an honest administrator finds many parallels in history. Two of our most honored American presidents were fiercely vilified when they were in office. The Philadelphia *Aurora*, on the morning of George Washington's retirement from office, proclaimed that "this day ought to be a Jubilee in the United States . . . for the man who is the source of all the misfortunes of our country, is this day reduced to a level with his fellow citizens."[2] Abraham Lincoln, one of the world's great heroes, was under a constant barrage of criticism in the country's newspapers. As late as June 9, 1864, less than a year before his assassination, the New York *World* attacked President Lincoln and Andrew Johnson:

> The age of statesmen is gone, the age of railsplitters and tailors, of buffoons, boors, and fanatics, has succeeded. . . . In a crisis of the most appalling magnitude, the country is asked to consider the claims of two ignorant, boorish, third-rate backwoods lawyers, for the highest stations in the government. . . . God save the Republic![3]

But we must not belabor the point. To emphasize only the abuse of an honest leader is to omit the most encouraging aspect of Joseph's tenure in Potiphar's house. Joseph was *a man blessed by God*. Jesus would later teach His disciples, "Blessed are you when men revile you and persecute you and utter all kinds of evil against you falsely on my account. Rejoice and be glad, for your reward is great in heaven" (Matthew 5:11, 12).

Joseph could have testified to the truth of Jesus' words. In everything that happened to him, he could see the providence of God. Notice these verses.

God blessed Joseph with success: "The Lord was with Joseph, and he became a successful man" (Genesis 39:2).

He blessed him with ability and prosperity: "And his master saw that the Lord was with him, and that the Lord caused all that he did to prosper in his hands" (verse 3).

He blessed the Egyptian through Joseph: "From the time that he made him overseer in his house and over all that he had the Lord blessed the Egyptian's house for Joseph's sake; the blessing of the Lord was upon all that he had" (verse 5).

He even blessed Joseph in prison: "But the Lord was with Joseph and showed him steadfast love, and gave him favor in the sight of the keeper of the prison" (verse 21).

Like the apostle Paul, Joseph had learned "in whatever state I am, to be content. I know how to be abased, and I know how to abound; in any and all circumstances I have learned the secret of facing plenty and hunger, abundance and want" (Philippians 4:11, 12). He was all wrapped up in God's blessings, wherever he was.

It could not always have seemed so. When Joseph was first thrown into prison, his future must have looked grim. But he had been in trouble before, and God had pulled him out. So he did not despair; instead, he allowed God to use his abilities to serve his fellow prisoners and assist the keeper of the prison. He later could thank God for this experience, because in prison he met the butler through whom he was to gain access to the Pharaoh. What had begun as a tragic chapter in Joseph's life ended in victory.

He was a man blessed by God, even in prison.

Charles Allen, the popular minister of America's largest Methodist Church, tells of the day when, eagerly preparing for his day's work, he felt a crippling pain in his back. His wife insisted that he see a doctor. The doctor immediately put Allen into the hospital and ordered him to stay there for a month. He was an unhappy, miserable patient, regretting the wasted time. But a dear minister friend of Allen called on him and said, "Charles, I have only one thing to say to you: 'He *maketh* me to lie down.' "

A good reminder. Sometimes in order to bless us God has to make us lie down. His providence sometimes leads us through the valley of the shadow of death, in order that at the end of the treacherous journey He can fill our cup to overflowing and keep us in His presence for ever and ever. Thanks to his friend, Allen could realize that the pauses, the detours, the setbacks on his journey could be means through which God would lead him to greater maturity and service.

"We know," the apostle Paul comforts us, "that in everything God works for good with those who love him, who are called according to his purpose" (Romans 8:28).

In everything.

Notes

¹Merle Miller, *Plain Speaking*, New York: Berkley Publishing Corporation, © 1973, 1974, p. 400.
²Samuel Morison, *History of the American People*. New York: Oxford University Press, 1965, p. 346.
³Quoted in Elton Trueblood, *The Life We Prize*. New York, Harper and Brothers, © 1951, p. 148.

In Spite of Everything, God Blesses

Genesis 48:1—16

Genesis, this amazingly modern book, has challenged us to rethink our faith in many ways, some of them disturbing. In this final chapter we now need to look back over our study to discover what, among the many valuable insights we have gained, is the overriding lesson of Genesis. Jacob (Israel) summarizes the Genesis message for us in his blessing to Joseph's sons (48:15, 16).

Israel assures Ephraim and Manasseh, and Genesis instructs us, that *God has a purpose for His people.* In the beginning God created the heavens and the earth and everything upon the earth. From the beginning He assigned man and woman purposeful activity. Be the image of God. Have dominion. Replenish the earth and subdue it. Keep the Garden of Eden.

But neither our first parents nor their descendants did their jobs very well. So God started all over again.

The new beginning is recorded in Genesis 12. God selected from among all humanity a people to be His very own. He called Abraham to leave His father's house and his kindred to journey to a strange land. In exchange for his obedience, God would prosper Abraham, making his descendants into a great nation, "and I will bless you, and make your name great, so that you will be a blessing." Read a restatement of the promise in Genesis 17:7, 8.

In the forty-eighth chapter, Israel, old, feeble, and blind, is preparing to die. He invokes God's special blessing upon his sons and grandsons. He does not hesitate to call upon his God because of God's promise to his father Isaac and his grandfather Abraham, and because of his own sense of God's protection in his life.

> The God before whom my fathers Abraham and
>   Isaac walked,
> the God who has led me all my life long to this
>   day,
> the angel who has redeemed me from all evil,
>   bless the lads . . .

To Abraham, to Isaac, and to Jacob there could be no doubt: God is, and He has a purpose for His people. Furthermore, He participates with His people in fulfilling His purpose. First He created them, then He chose them to be His own. Always He loves them, sometimes He judges them, and if necessary He rescues them.

It is this sense of belonging to a purposeful God that Jacob hands on to his descendants with his blessing. A father reading this passage cannot help wondering what, when the time comes, he will hand down to his heirs. Will he leave a good name, a reputation, or maybe money? Will his God be their God, to bless them as He has blessed him, overseeing, comforting, caring for them? This certainly is Israel's desire. He wants his heirs to know that God has a purpose for His people.

Not everyone believes that God is so involved with us. Some time ago a man was sitting beside his fireplace watching a new litter of pups while they stumbled and tumbled and fell over one another. A bemused smile covered his face as he fancied himself to be something like God looking down on men tumbling and stumbling and falling over one another. But he was wrong. The God of Abraham and Isaac and Jacob is not an aloof, detached being who watches passively from afar. Instead, he journeys with Abraham, wrestles with Jacob, and rescues a famine-stricken population through Joseph. He is not an aloof God, but an involved one.

The ancient Hebrews were convinced that their God works with His people according to His purposes and for their good. This unshakable conviction accounts for the vigor and courage that have long distinguished them. The same belief has characterized Christian heroes. It emboldened the apostles, with their lives in danger, to defy their captors: "We must obey God rather than men" (Acts 5:29). Stephen was unafraid of the raging mob and faced his death with tranquility. He could not be shaken, because even at the end he knew God was working through him; his vision of Christ standing at the right hand of God was the final evidence that God approved his boldness (Acts 7:56). Paul's "I can do all things in him who strengthens me" (Philippians 4:13) was spoken by one whose every action was in obedience to "Christ who lives in me" (Galatians 2:20). Martin Luther's famous "Here I stand" is the epitome of courage in the face of danger. It was said by a seventeenth-century observer, "I'd rather meet coming against me a whole regiment with drawn swords than one Calvinist convinced that he is doing the will of God."

To leap from the seventeenth to the twentieth century forces us to ask, If it was true for our ancestors, is it true for us? Do we believe that God still has a purpose for His people? If so, are we in harmony with it? If we are, then the conviction, power, energy, enthusiasm, and courage we see in Biblical believers will certainly be ours. The assertion, however, leads directly to the second major lesson from Genesis.

Even though God does have a purpose for His people, *they do not always do His will*. I wish it were otherwise. I wish that from the moment God called Abraham, the earth could have boasted of one group among all the groups of mankind that was better than the others, so much better that it could be said, "They are God's people. You can tell it by the way they act." But Genesis is too honest to make that claim. Prior to Abraham there were Adam and Eve, rebelling against God's authority. Then Cain and Abel and the first murder. Then the contemporaries of Noah, whose every imagination of the heart was wicked. Then the arrogant builders of Babel's tower. In the Genesis account the twelfth chapter marks a new beginning, with God seizing the initiative and selecting His people. And we hope for something better from humanity. But you know the rest of the story. Even Abraham was flawed, as were Isaac and Jacob and all their families. There was none righteous, no not one.

In Genesis 34 there is the particularly horrible story of Dinah. Shechem violated her innocence, it is true; but he tried to correct the wrong by making her his wife. Negotiations between his family and Jacob's were successfully concluded when Simeon and Levi, Jacob's sons, broke the family's word and slaughtered Shechem and his people, stealing all their wealth and capturing the women and children. Mass murder, committed by the people of God!

You cannot read Genesis and conclude that God's people always do God's will. The record makes it plain that they do not.

If we become personal we can understand the problem. I'm a child of God, a Christian. I am proud to be a member of the church, proud to wear the name Christian. But I am not proud of all this Christian does. In spite of my knowledge of God's will for my life—to be truthful, upright, just, kind, gentle, patient, etc.—I seldom live up to what I know. I wish it were otherwise, especially in light of Jesus' explicit appeal, "You, therefore, must be perfect, as your heavenly Father is perfect" (Matthew 5:48).

I'm not. Are you?

I sometimes think the problem is that we don't want to be good. There are some people who can't be made good because they don't want to be. Like Lucy in *Peanuts*. One day she slammed the door as she came into the room and announced, "Boy, do I feel crabby." Linus, concerned about her, offered to help. He gave her his place before the television, fixed her a nice sandwich and some chocolate cookies and a glass of milk. Then he wanted to know if there was anything else he could get, anything he hadn't thought of. And Lucy told him. "Yes, there is one thing you haven't thought of. I don't want to feel better!"

There are days like that for all of us, when we don't want to feel better and don't want to do better. Sometimes we dignify our stubbornness by insisting that we don't really know the will of God. If we are honest, however, we admit that knowledge is not the problem, but willfulness. We resemble the old man who had grown tired of living. His friends had died, his family was gone, and little was left for him but to grumble to his visitors, "I don't know why God doesn't just take me." One caller answered him. "Maybe it's because He still has work for you to do here on earth." "Well," said the old man, "I'm not going to do it."

Like the old man, God's people are not always willing to cooperate with the purpose of God. They talk about His will. They even pray about it. But they don't always do it.

This fact, however, leads us to the most glorious message of Genesis. *In spite of everything that His people do, God remains faithful.* He wants to bless.

Here is Jacob, an ancient man marshalling his nearly exhausted strength to sit up in bed to bless his grandsons. I wonder whether he thought it rather presumptuous, knowing his family's record—and his own less than spotless character. The records are not good. But in spite of everything, he still dares to ask God to bless his family. He believes they will grow into a great nation, not because they deserve it, certainly not because they have always done God's will, but because God keeps His word.

Frankly, that's our only hope also. On the day when our records are examined, who can boast of his own or his family's history? "Let him who boasts boast of the Lord" (1 Corinthians 1:31).

A good friend of mine spent a year in prison. After a distinguished career as a Christian minister and professor, he experienced the humiliation of being convicted and sentenced for a felony. He now speaks of the year in jail as the best one in his life. While still in jail he wrote,

> All these experiences are stripping from me a good deal of the unreal that has stuck to me like a plague all my life. And in this I can rejoice. I needed to find out that God as a moral God, good and loving, will not tolerate wrong (even wrong judgments) in His own children. But neither does He abandon them or forsake them. And He certainly never holds over them the blackmail of a "record."[1]

In spite of everything, God blesses.

Jacob says that the God before whom Abraham and Isaac walked "has *led* me all my life long to this day." The King James Version reads "has *fed*." The word means *shepherded*. The God who has led me beside still waters and made me lie down in green pastures, who has protected me from wild animals and kept me safe—this God I am asking to bless my children.

"The Lord is my shepherd," sings the psalmist (Psalm 23). God is like a good shepherd, Jesus teaches, who will leave the ninety and nine and seek to save the lost one (Luke 15). The missing one may have wandered aimlessly away, or he may have deliberately left the group, or may have carelessly caught himself in a bramble. But whatever the cause, and in spite of everything, the Good Shepherd seeks to save him.

In everything God works for good with those who love him, who are called according to his purpose (Romans 8:28).

This then is the message of Genesis: God wants to bless His people. Therefore we can say even today, as Jacob could say to his grandsons,

In spite of my personal record
    in spite of the blotches on our family record
        in spite of our unworthiness before His
            holy presence,
                in spite of everything,
                    God bless you.

Notes
[1] Owen Crouch, *Dear Lorna*. New York: Carlton Press, © 1974, pp. 12, 13.